"There is healing and hope in this book for everyone damaged by a selfish dad. God will surely use this book greatly."

—Stephen Arterburn
Founder, New Life Ministries

"As the leader of a women's ministry, I have seen firsthand the toll taken in a woman's life when the relationship with her father has been damaged because her father hasn't 'been there.' Whether a woman experiences father loss due to death, divorce, emotional unavailability, abandonment, or any number of other reasons, the effect on her life can be devastating. Using scriptural wisdom and practical experience, Norman Wright offers hope and help to those women. I believe nearly every woman will be able to relate to the stories shared in this book and will find encouragement in her journey of healing and wholeness."

—Jane Hansen
President/CEO, Aglow International

Books by
H. Norman Wright

FROM BETHANY HOUSE PUBLISHERS

The Complete Book of Christian Wedding Vows

Healing for the Father Wound

The Perfect Catch

H. NORMAN WRIGHT

HEALING
FOR THE
FATHER
WOUND

~

A TRUSTED CHRISTIAN COUNSELOR

OFFERS TIME-TESTED ADVICE

BETHANYHOUSE
MINNEAPOLIS, MINNESOTA

Published by Bethany House Publishers
11400 Hampshire Avenue South
Bloomington, Minnesota 55438

Bethany House Publishers is a division of
Baker Publishing Group, Grand Rapids, Michigan.

Printed in the United States of America

In keeping with biblical principles of creation stewardship, Baker Publishing Group advocates the responsible use of our natural resources. As a member of the Green Press Initiative, our company uses recycled paper when possible. The text paper of this book is comprised of 30% post-consumer waste.

Library of Congress Cataloging-in-Publication Data

Wright, H. Norman.
    [Dad-shaped hole in my heart]
    Healing the father wound: a trusted Christian counselor offers time-tested advice / by H. Norman Wright.
    p. cm.
    Originally published: A dad-shaped hole in my heart. Minneapolis, Minn. : Bethany House Publishers, c2005.
    Summary: "Words of caring and restoration for women whose dads were missing from their lives—whether emotionally, physically, or spiritually"—Provided by publisher.
    Includes bibliographical references.
    ISBN 978-0-7642-0535-4 (pbk. : alk. paper)
    1. Christian women—Religious life. 2. God (Christianity)—Fatherhood. 3. Fathers—Death—Religious aspects—Christianity. 4. Loss (Psychology)—Religious aspects—Christianity. 5. Paternal deprivation—Religious aspects—Christianity. 6. Absentee fathers. 7. Fathers and daughters. I. Title.
    BV4527.W68   2008
    248.8'43—dc22   2008001692

H. NORMAN WRIGHT is a licensed marriage, family, and child therapist, as well as a certified trauma specialist. A graduate of Westmont College, Fuller Theological Seminary, and Pepperdine University, Dr. Wright has received two honorary doctorates from Western Conservative Baptist Seminary and Biola University. He has taught at the graduate level at both Biola University and Talbot Seminary. At the present time he is research professor of Christian education at Talbot School of Theology.

He is the author of more than 70 books, including *Helping Those Who Hurt, The Perfect Catch,* and *The Complete Book of Christian Wedding Vows*. Dr. Wright has pioneered premarital counseling programs throughout the country and conducts seminars on many subjects, including marriage enrichment, parenting, and grief recovery. His current focus is in crisis and trauma counseling and critical incident debriefings within the wider community.

His hobbies include bass fishing, gardening, and training his golden retriever, Shadow, as a therapy response dog. Norm was married for forty-seven years to his wife, Joyce, who died in 2007. He resides in Bakersfield, California.

CONTENTS

INTRODUCTION

Who you are today was shaped by your father. He continues to influence you. He may have been a central part of your life, or he might have been absent. He could exist only in your mind, or you may be talking to him every day. You may be searching for your dad, or his substitute, in relationships with other men. No matter how old you are, it's important to understand your father's influence upon your life.

As I see it, picking up this book is an act of courage on your part. Whether it's because of heart issues with your own dad, or dad problems faced by someone you care about, you are looking for answers, and I know that can be a potentially frightening and painful process. To open up old wounds and clean them out isn't fun. But this book is designed to provide everything you need to find healing and a new start with God.

You are not alone. Many people struggle with problems—both physical and emotional—that are directly related to their relationship with their earthly father. In this book you'll read testimonies of other women who have experienced many of the hurts you have and still ache with the disappointment of a failed relationship with their dad. You'll also hear how some gained victory over their emotionally crushing situations.

You'll have the opportunity to work through your own particular issues in the exercises provided in some of the chapters. I recommend that you take the time to carefully consider and then put down in words your unique experiences. You will be amazed at how helpful it is to articulate your feelings and to put into practice some of the suggestions that follow. If you don't bypass these helpful exercises, I know your healing will happen much faster.

As a Christian therapist I have seen the devastation that results from failed human relationships. This is why I have written this book. I want to see you and many like you set free from the pain of all that. Over the years I have come to understand how important it is for us to be willing to face the things that we don't even want to admit are in us. I want to help you understand the impact that your dad had on your life (for good or bad) and show you how the experiences you had with him have influenced some of the choices you make as an adult. Even the way you view life is in large part the result of your family interactions and experiences.

In my counseling practice I have also had the opportunity to watch as God, our heavenly Father, has touched individual hearts who were brave enough to face their pain. I have seen Him restore what looked like a hopeless situation with His special power and grace. And even when the relationship between the woman and her father could not be restored, I have seen God meet her deepest needs and heal the hurt in her heart in a way she could not have envisioned.

This is sometimes a long and lonely battle that you wage. But don't give up hope. You *can* find a better life in spite of any and all problems that your earthly father may have brought into your life. The key is to discover that all along your heavenly Father was aware of you and longing to replace what was lost. It is never too late. New life beckons beyond the present pain you feel. Don't let your past disappointments spoil the rest of your life.

I hope the following chapters will not only give you a glimpse into the kinds of problems that can arise when your earthly father fails you but also give concrete help in overcoming them. The good news is that no hurt or disappointment can defeat us if we put our trust in someone else who *is* perfect and loves us unconditionally: our heavenly Father. My earnest prayer for this book is that it will lead you to Him.

Chapter 1

HEART PROBLEMS

———

I'd like to begin this first chapter with June's story. In many ways her story mirrors the cry of countless daughters just like you, who struggle with the effects of a dad who wasn't there for them. Year after year they cry: *Daddy, where are you? Who are you?*

My son was born five years ago. He's a healthy, energetic child. At least he appeared to be healthy at birth. But a few days later we discovered he had a defect. It wasn't visible. No one could see it. But it was there, and it was serious. *He had a hole in his heart.* He was born that way. Within a week after we discovered it, the doctors opened his chest and repaired that hole in his little heart. He was able to go on with his life in a normal manner. He's not even aware that he had a hole in his heart.

I wish I could say the same. My son and I are alike. We've both had holes in our heart. He was born that way and it was repaired. I wasn't born with one, but over my childhood years the hole was created and it grew larger as I grew. It hasn't been repaired, even though I've tried. It's a different shape than my son's. The hole in my heart is *in the shape of my father*. Physical surgery won't repair the hole. It will take something like emotional surgery or healing for it to slowly close. I'm not sure how to go about the process. I'm confused. Is it dependent upon my father reaching into my life and somehow undoing what he did or doing what he failed to do years ago? I just want a whole heart. It's too bad there are no heart transplants for this kind of disorder.

There are many daughters who are missing something from their father that should have been given. Or he responded to them in ways that were way beyond what any daughter should have to endure. Or he simply vanished one day from their lives and hasn't reappeared. Any of these experiences can create a hole that seemingly cannot be filled by anything else. If you think you are alone, that your pain is unique to you and your family, I hope that this book will show you that this is not true. Listen in as other adult daughters share how their dads influenced them—sometimes positively and sometimes negatively—far beyond their childhood years.

My relationship with my father was incomplete, guarded, confusing, and sad. He was an intelligent, funny, deep, and personally likable man when sober, and an explosive, unpredictable, abusive, angry, pathetic, destructive shell of a man when drinking, which increased as time went on.

My father and I have always had a good relationship. He has always held high standards, but they were never unreasonable. I hold those same standards today—expectations that people should always try their best, be polite, behave themselves, and make something of themselves, but also not to allow ambition to get in the way of happiness. I can talk to my father about anything and feel very comfortable asking his advice on things relating to finances, politics, and life in general. We have grown closer as I have gotten older because we share the same love of history and good conversation about important things, plus we both have grown spiritually over the past five to ten years. I have never felt anything but good about our relationship in general, though of course there were times when we may not have seen eye to eye, as there are in any father/daughter relationship.

My father was not available for me emotionally. I do not recall ever discussing struggles or problems with him or seeking his counsel. I recall asking his advice about a boyfriend once when I was in college. I had consciously decided to offer him the opportunity to give me advice because I had been thinking that maybe he hadn't given any counsel because I had never asked. I remember his responding that he really couldn't answer the question, and that I would need to decide, because it was my life. (It was apparent that he was not comfortable with giving me advice.) He was not available to help with homework or provide advice on anything like choosing classes, extracurricular activity options, career possibilities, my interests or life goals, moral decisions, college options, car repairs, home purchases. Although I performed well in school (A & B honor rolls) and was/am extremely responsible, I do not recall my dad offering praise or acknowledgment other than on very rare occasions, and only as a result of my mom's prompting. (On a positive note, I know that as an adult, he is proud of me and I do know that he loves me. I observe that he asks questions about things in my life and is trying to get to know me. I am touched by these things.)

My biological father was in my life from birth till I was approximately six and a half years old. I came five years after the loss of a two-year-old daughter. My dad spoiled me, carried me in his arms or on his shoulders. He was kind, loving, indulgent, and oh so strong. At six-and-a-half my dad had a breakdown, and I didn't see him again until I was fourteen. By then I didn't know him and was afraid.

The gap between my father and me is actually growing as we get older. I'm beginning to see how disrespectful and hurtful he can be and has been in the past toward my mom. I'm having a hard time reconciling the daddy I loved as a child and the man that I recognize him to be today. I'm embarrassed by some of the things he does, but I still want to defend him to the grave. It's painful.

My father wasn't there for me. Until I was thirteen, he was gone from early in the morning, after breakfast, till dinner time . . . to work mostly. When he was home, he retreated into a book or turned on the radio. We kids were to be seen and not heard. He played music or the news during meals. Then the summer I turned thirteen he left us, at our mom's request. She said later that she couldn't take his criticism and silence. I was relieved. My brother was angry. He said that ended his hope of having a dad like everyone else. I was glad that I didn't have to pretend to sleep in on the weekends to avoid his anger. When I was engaged and brought my intended to meet him, Dad refused to shake hands with him. He stood there with his arms folded over his chest and told my fiancé that some people worked, and those who couldn't work were teachers. My fiancé was a teacher.

Because my father was an alcoholic, it was almost like having two fathers. When he was sober he was loving and fun. When he was drunk I became the adult, since he became the one who needed to be taken care of.

It was a wonderful, close relationship. His love and respect for my mother was the greatest gift a man can give his family. Although I grew up during the Depression, I never doubted that he would take care of me. He was well respected in our community, and I felt it a privilege to be his daughter.

Father—a powerful word. A positive word for some and painful for others. What is a father? *Who* is he supposed to be, and *what* is he supposed to do? Sometimes in my counseling practice I have heard women describe what they wish their fathers would be or had been, and my only response has been, "He doesn't exist anywhere." He sounded like Superfather, who could bound from one building to another. Some create fathers in the image of what they want him to be rather than what he could ever be. Often we do this with God, our heavenly Father, too.

As I work with those in grief and trauma, I'm often given a window to look through into a person's theology. What we believe about God really comes to the forefront when we are hurting. And so often what I hear is what people wish God would be rather than who He is according to the Scriptures. But we cannot create God in the image we want Him to be in order to satisfy our needs. He is who He is, whether that meets our approval or not.

In the same way, some women will never have the father they want, not because of a deficiency in their dad but because what they desire is unrealistic and unattainable. For others, what they want is reasonable, and it would be healthier for their dad if he *were* that way. But some fathers are so emotionally and/or developmentally challenged it would take years of work—maybe even therapy—for his healing to occur. Only then could his daughter hope to see the preferred change in their father-daughter relationship.

The book *The Wonder of Girls—Understanding the Hidden Nature of Our Daughters* by Michael Gurian[1] is one of the best books I've seen on this topic. In a very succinct way the author describes the impact of a father on his daughter. He says,

> A father who is honest with his daughter about his own flaws becomes her confidant. A father who remains stoic becomes her enigma to solve. A father who distances himself too greatly from his daughter becomes a burden she carries into life. If a father always finds time to cuddle, listen to, toss in the air, dance with, run alongside, coach, comfort, and protect his daughter, he will give her the gift of life he is built

to give. If a father withholds nothing, teaching his daughter the life skills she needs to know, he shares an active kind of respect for variety in a girl's developing self. If a father competes with his daughter in games, but especially when she is young lets her win her share of races, he is showing her both his own humility and her potential. And as a father helps a daughter enter the worlds of sexuality, romance, and then marriage, a man becomes more than an arm to walk down the aisle with—he becomes, in his daughter's mind, fearless. . . .

How I Saw Him

It may help to understand how your father impacted you if you can remember how you viewed him at different stages in your childhood. Can you remember what you thought and felt about your father at the following ages?

Age 3 _____

_____

Age 6 _____

_____

Age 9 _____

_____

Age 12 _____

_____

I've seen a number of individuals and friends over the years with a wide variety of heart problems. Some have irregularities in their heartbeats; others have a too-rapid heartbeat. In some cases the problem can be corrected with medication, but sometimes a pacemaker must be installed. Others I have known have experienced heart failure and heart strain because of blocked arteries. One friend who experienced all the classic signs of a heart attack finally went to his doctor to find that it was a wonder he was still walking around—two of his arteries were 100 percent blocked and another had 90-percent blockage. He immediately underwent heart surgery for a quintuple bypass.

Some people have to have a complete heart transplant to get on with life.

COMMON HEART PROBLEMS IN DAUGHTERS

Just as our physical pump called the heart can have numerous problems that have to be corrected by doctors, so our emotional lives can suffer from various maladies of the heart that arise because of our faulty relationships.

1. The bruised heart. A daughter with a bruised heart feels beaten down. She feels she can never be good enough to live up to the expectations of those around her, especially her father. Much of the time she feels ashamed, fearful, and insecure. It hurts too much to try, so the fear of making a mistake or losing makes her reluctant to enter wholeheartedly into life.

She lives in a survival mode, believing, "I have to look out for myself because no one else will. And if they say they will, I can't depend upon them." Withdrawing is one way to protect herself and eliminate being hurt. Often she is very sensitive, and at times despair and hopelessness are her companions.

A woman with a bruised heart came into being because she didn't receive approval, validation, sufficient attention, or support from important people in her life. Either her father didn't know how to give this, made it conditional, wasn't around to give it, or chose not to give it. And these four crucial elements (approval, validation, attention, and support) become like a quest to such a daughter. Often the way she goes about trying to find these is unhealthy, creating other problems for her, or she self-sabotages her efforts.

What I would like you to know right at the start of this book is that there is hope for an aching heart. Jesus Christ is and has the answer for a bruised heart, for He is "gentle and humble in heart" (Matthew 11:29). A prophet said of Jesus, "A bruised reed he will not break, and a smoldering wick he will not snuff out" (Matthew 12:20). He wants bruised daughters to remember: *It's all right if everything isn't all right. You can be all right even if your father wasn't all right.* There is a God who is there and will provide for you. He does care and He does heal hearts that are bruised.

2. *The performance heart.* There is a heart problem that at first glance doesn't appear to be a problem. It belongs to the daughter who drives herself to be the best in whatever it is that she does. The fear of failure and disappointment is her driving force. For some it's the message to her father, "I'll show you. I can be successful.

THERE IS HOPE FOR AN ACHING HEART.

I can be the best. You didn't give me what I needed, so I'll get it myself." And to add to the feelings of inadequacy, she's selective in her search for approval. Often she seeks only those with status, who can validate how well she's done. What drives a daughter in this way? Doubt. Feelings of inadequacy. The I-don't-measure-up-in-the-eyes-of-my-dad syndrome. She invests her identity in how well she performs, with the thought drumming through her mind, "I can and I will do it." Unfortunately, this heart has to continually do *more* and perform *better* in order to be valued.

Jesus would say, *It's not necessary.* He values you for who you are. It's not based on your performance. God does not love you for what you do. You can't perform well enough in anything to earn His love. God both wants you to say and enables you to say, "It's all right that I'm not perfect. God sees me as perfect in Christ. I don't have to prove anything to my father. He isn't the ultimate judge of my value."

3. *The hardened heart.* I've seen hearts that are hard—like concrete. This problem is a clear sign of tremendous hurt in the father-daughter relationship. In this case a daughter has been hurt so much by life that she shuts down emotionally and cuts herself off from her heart. She thinks, "If you feel, you hurt, so block the feelings—stuff them." The one emotion she allows herself to feel is anger, and it comes out quite strongly. Often the approval and protection she wanted as a child never came, and that disappointment produced the hurt in her. But this daughter can learn that disappointments are a part of life. God is the author of feelings, and it's all right to experience the entire range of emotions. God is there to assist us in whatever our feelings might be. Rather than stuff them, she has to come to terms with what happened and accepts her hurt as a legitimate response to her experience. Only then can she begin to heal and feel her heart soften.

4. The addicted heart is another hurting heart. It's a heart that latches onto people, activities, substances, food, anything that will cover the hurt inside. Everything is done in excess in order to cover the disappointments of life. But unfortunately it doesn't work. It's a substitute that doesn't live up to its promises. The hurts and the hole are still there. It's an attempt to cope that fails. It's an escape that leads back into the prison. The neediness can only be satisfied when the love and message of Jesus—"You're all right"—finds a home in your heart.[2]

A SCRIPTURAL LOOK AT YOUR HEART

Your heart is extremely important. Much of what we eat is selected because of how it will affect our heart. We exercise because the heart is one of the organs of the body that benefits most from it. In Scripture, the heart is referred to again and again, but it is not referring to the physical organ.

In the Hebrew language the heart is the center of the being and the intellect. It's with your heart that you feel, perceive, make moral choices. It's your heart that searches after God and responds to Him. Take a look at how the Old Testament Scriptures use the word. Since your heart is the organ of "feeling," it despairs, grieves, is filled with terror, is sad, or cheerful. Discouragement is to "lose heart" and anger makes the heart "grow hot." (See Deuteronomy 28:65; 1 Samuel 2:33; 17:32; 28:5; Nehemiah 2:2; Psalm 39:3; 119:111; Proverbs 17:22.)

Your heart is also the center of your perceptual, or thinking, life. The Scripture states that your heart knows things, it discerns, and it has wisdom. It is the place where the Word of God is to be stored so that by understanding what God wants you won't sin against him (Deuteronomy 4:39; 8:5; 1 Kings 3:9; 10:24; Psalm 119:11).

Your heart is the organ of moral choice, and the Scripture is quite explicit about that. Jesus said, "Out of the *heart* come evil thoughts, murder, adultery, sexual immorality, theft, false testimony, slander" (Matthew 15:19, emphasis added). But on the other side of the coin, the heart can be upright, steadfast, and full of integrity (Psalm 97:11; 108:1; 1 Kings 9:4).

We are all asked to love God with all our heart. Your heart could be hard, or committed to Him. It can see God, or be enticed away from Him. It can be unrepentant and unbelieving, or sincere in its faith (Exodus 8:32; 2 Chronicles 15:17; 19:3; Job 31:9; Romans 2:5; Hebrews 10:22). But no matter what type of father you had or what your experiences were with him, you have tremendous value, worth, and significance. Consider these words:

> You are not an accident. Your birth was no mistake or mishap, and your life is no fluke of nature. . . . Long before you were conceived by your parents, you were conceived in the mind of God. He thought of you first. . . . He custom-made your body just the way He wanted it. He also determined the natural talents you would possess and the uniqueness of your personality. . . . Most amazing, God decided *how* you would be born. Regardless of the circumstance of your birth or who your parents are, God had a plan in creating you. It doesn't matter whether your parents were good, bad or indifferent. God knew that those two individuals possessed exactly the right genetic makeup to create the custom "you" he had in mind. They had the DNA God wanted to make you. . . . God never does anything accidentally, and He never makes mistakes—He has a reason for everything He creates. . . . God was thinking of you even

before he made the world. . . . This is how much God loves and values you.[3]

Read that paragraph once every day, out loud, for one month. You will be amazed at the difference it will make in your life.

Our Unique Stories

As I approached this book, I wanted it to be more than a source of information and helps. I wanted it to be an opportunity for adult daughters to tell their stories. Many have never shared their experiences in an in-depth manner before. Some were hesitant to do so, since the pain of their losses was reactivated. For others, it was more of a positive reflection, since they were fortunate enough to have had a father who responded as a father should. Hopefully their stories will help you to look closely into your own experience. Perhaps you had a good father-daughter relationship, or you could be like the quiet multitude of women who carry an empty place in their heart where Dad should have been.

We asked women from across the country to complete a questionnaire of just nine questions in order to gather insights into the unique and very important relationship between a daughter and her earthly father.

After reading these stories, spend some time reflecting on them, then give your answers before proceeding. These may be questions you've never considered before, but hopefully they'll help you understand yourself—and your father—in a new way.

Here are the nine questions we asked in the survey:

1. How would you describe your relationship with your father?
2. In what way was your father there for you?
3. In what way wasn't your father there for you?
4. Describe how your father has influenced or shaped your life (either negatively or positively).
5. If your relationship was lacking, what have you done to overcome this?

6. What do you appreciate the most *and* the least in your father's involvement with you?
7. If your father's interaction was missing in your life, how did you fill this void?
8. How has your relationship with your earthly father affected your relationship with God and with Jesus?
9. At this point in your life, what would you like to be able to say to your father?

Here are the responses from two women:

How would you describe your relationship with your father?

"He was controlling, a perfectionist, military man, and unfortunately, an alcoholic. I was fearful of him, yet wanting to have his approval and love. My sister, mother, and I were all afraid of him. For example, he would come up to my room with white gloves on and check for dust and then try to bounce a quarter off my bed! I can laugh about it now, but back then, we lived waiting for the other shoe to drop. My father was sexually abusive with me as well. It is difficult to put into words the ambivalence I felt toward him. I loved him, yet hated what he was doing to me."

In what way wasn't your father there for you?

"He was emotionally absent, except in inappropriate ways, meaning, he would ask me, 'Do you love me?' then, 'Tell me you love me. If you love me you wouldn't go out with your friends— you would stay with me.' He was not there as a provider of safety. I felt fearful around him, especially when my sister and mother were gone. My dad did not know how to offer unconditional love or acceptance. Anything he gave to me had a price tag. Offerings of stuffed animals were bribes, not gifts, and I was embarrassed when he bought me things (such as a very expensive bracelet)."

Describe how your father has influenced or shaped your life (negatively or positively).

"Negative: I had no concept of healthy boundaries, therefore, relationships were unhealthy (I did not know where I stopped and others began). Only by the grace of God my husband and I have been married twenty-eight years. Spiritually, I struggled in believing in God because my father was a Sunday school teacher and deacon in our church. Emotionally, I was fragile. I had to work hard to overcome many fears throughout my life (fears of being raped, being alone, rejection, abandonment). For many years I was filled with constant worry, always on the alert. I know now that even my brain was affected due to the trauma. Through many years of Christian counseling, God has paved *new* pathways in my brain, rather than remaining stuck in fear and insecurity. And intimacy was something else that needed to receive the healing touch of God.

"Positive: I knew I had to work hard to survive in life."

If your relationship was lacking, what have you done to overcome this?

"I became a Christian at the age of thirty, and God began a healing process in my life (in every way . . . spiritually, emotionally, mentally, relationally, physically). After years of physical illness and depression, I started counseling, and God used what man has meant for evil and turned it for good. I slowly was able to face the truth of my past, the *truth* of His Word, and the truth of my own heart condition. God did exceedingly abundantly more than I could have ever imagined. *He* is my all in all, my every breath, my living water, my daily bread, my healing and sustaining grace, the lover of my soul, the lifter of my head, and the author and perfecter of my faith. Praise God. All I have experienced has been used for His glory and to equip me to fulfill His purpose. Now I am a Christian counselor, offering the comfort to others that God gave to me. *This* is the abundant life. As my parents both battled cancer at the same time, I was able to care for them and offer them Christ's love."

How has your relationship with your earthly father affected your relationship with God and with Jesus?

"I definitely had a difficult time relating to Father God. I did not like to read the Old Testament for many, many years. But Jesus' love melted my heart, and as He continued to heal me, my heart was opened to my heavenly Father."

At this point in your life, what would you like to be able to say to your father?

"He and my mom died two years ago. I was able to tell him several times before he died (we had reconciled two years before his cancer), that I forgave him as my Jesus had forgiven me. We prayed together, took care of my mother together. God gave me the privilege to pray with my mother and she accepted the Lord, and my dad told me he had already done so. I believe he did. I know I will see him in heaven just the way God created him to be . . . the way he was before his woundedness. If I could talk with him, I guess I would say, 'I wish you could have loved me with a godly love, and cherished me as a little girl should be cherished. I would have loved to feel safe sitting on your lap.'"

Another woman responded to these same questions:

How would you describe your relationship with your father?

"As a little girl I was terrified of my father. He often took out his anger on me. If he had a bad day, he would come home and beat me up. He would also tell me things that hurt me deeply—that I was worthless, ugly, stupid. He also sexually abused me, beginning when I was a little girl (my first memory is in kindergarten) until I left his house at eighteen years old."

In what way was your father there for you?

"My mind is blank with this. I know he provided for us, but when I was sixteen I had to rent a car if I was to use it, pay for gas, and buy my clothes. He also threatened to charge me rent, even though he made very good money. The only thing I can give him credit for is that he told me what was wrong with me and taught me how to work hard."

In what way wasn't your father there for you?

"He gave me no positive emotional support. He didn't encourage my femininity; I was petrified to be a woman around him. I was very scared when I began my period because I felt the sexual abuse would increase. I also was afraid for him to see I was developing. I hid in big clothes. I became very afraid of older men and what they would do to me. He never protected me. When I hinted that the neighbor was touching me in bad places he told me I was lying. My brother also sexually abused me and he did nothing to protect me. When I became pregnant from the neighbor boy he told me to have an abortion, and paid for it. Neither he (nor my mother) did anything when I bled a lot from the abortion; they just forced me to go to school. I could not talk to them or let them know what I thought in any way. I was taught not to be a person, but to be only what they wanted me to be. He controlled me in every way—whenever I showed him in any way that I had a personality beyond his control he became very violent, sometimes smashing my head into the fireplace until I blacked out, or putting scars on my body with a belt or his fists."

Describe how your father has influenced or shaped your life (either negatively or positively).

HE TAUGHT ME HOW TO HATE MYSELF.

"He taught me how to hate myself, my body, hate that I was a woman and that I was his daughter. He also taught me to be very promiscuous because that was the only way he showed me any caring; he would tell me he loved me when he became sexual with me. He taught me how to be afraid all of the time and to work hard to show him I was perfect so he wouldn't beat me up. I think he influenced me positively because I have put the negative into the hands of God and constantly asked God how to turn this around to good. God has taught me how to work hard to find who I am in Him. I believe to the depths of my heart that God is my Father, and I am adopted by Him. God has also put many positive fatherly men in my life. It has taken me a long time to trust them, but they have shaped me in many positive ways."

If your relationship was lacking, what have you done to overcome this?

"I am dependent on who I am in Christ. I see myself as a cherished daughter of my Abba Father. I am also a very passionate person. I desperately want to be healthy and have a pure heart so I can teach others to do the same. I have tried to be successful and educated, everything my earthly father taught me that I am not. It has been a battle to realize that I am not stupid, ugly, and worthless, to escape self-condemnation."

If your father's interaction was missing in your life, how did you fill this void?

"When I was twenty years old my father and mother told me, 'As far we are concerned you don't exist.' They also legally disowned me. This was a real blow and shattered my world, but in many ways it was a blessing because I let go of them, their abusive words, and began to pick my life up after a few years. This was mainly because I became a Christian and God began to father me."

At this point in your life, what would you like to be able to say to your father?

"I love you, I forgive you, I long to see you in heaven with me. I had to let go of my anger toward you because it was hurting me too much—I wish you could experience the grace and forgiveness from God as I have. He is waiting for you and desires to give it to you."

The women who wrote these responses are survivors. They experienced intense pain and betrayal and yet found healing. Some have asked, "How could anyone overcome some of those experiences? How can you survive such abuse?" Some readers will fixate on the pain—while others will see the redemption.

Remember, these recoveries were journeys. They didn't happen overnight. You may already be on your own journey, or you may need to begin. In either case, be aware that these victories are gained a step at a time. It's slow, but the good news is that victory is *possible*.

As you continue through this book, read for understanding as well as discovering steps to take to heal the hole in your heart. Don't compare your responses and reactions with anyone else's. What many aren't aware of is the fact that an inadequate or absent father created losses in your life, and any loss requires a grieving process. Expect that to occur. Welcome it, in fact, because grief is the road to recovery. It enables you to move on with your life.

Chapter 2

A FATHER'S PERSPECTIVE

What is it like to be a father? Have you ever looked at the task through the eyes of your father? He sees things differently than you do. Men like to be in charge and in control. Regardless of what you see and hear from your father, he's not as confident about this "thing" called fathering as you may think. One dad wrote:

> I'm really struggling with the fact that I don't think that I verbalize how wonderful my daughters are often enough. I do tell them, but it does not flow spontaneously from my being. I don't have the training or the modeling for it. I'll say, "Good job!" but I also don't want it to be a "job." You know—the idea that you have value because you did something. That has been my toughest thing. Maybe just sitting with them with my arm around them, maybe that's telling them how special they are to me. I'm not sure. I have very little confidence about myself.[1]

Men struggle with a father-to-daughter relationship. One man said, "I'm just not sure what a father to a daughter is supposed to do or be. How would I know since I was a son?" Many of the hurdles they face exist in their thoughts and come out of the anxiety of feeling they are not in control, like they would like to be.

Every father, unfortunately, has to find his own way in being a father. Who has ever taken the time to teach a man to be a father—especially the father of a daughter? Our first child was a daughter, Sheryl. I had questions, especially since I was like many men. I didn't have any sisters. My experience with girls was limited. How do you know what to do or say? It was a constant state of learning for me.

MANY MEN STRUGGLE WITH THE ROLE OF FATHERING.

Many men struggle with the role of fathering, especially with the other gender. A mother's involvement with a baby is different because there's a very different type of bonding occurring. A mother's attachment is easier since she has higher doses of oxytocin, progesterone, or estrogen—the biochemicals that help to form personal attachments. Your father, on the other hand, had to rely on emotional and social bonding with you. This is sometimes difficult since so many of us men are emotionally challenged in the first place. Generally speaking we have less inclination for emotional connection than women do, and then we often are not taught how to respond emotionally during our upbringing. We lack a basic feelings vocabulary. "How do I talk 'emotionally'?" is the struggle of many men.

We fathers, more than mothers, have to "learn to father." It doesn't come as naturally. A father needs to be attached to his daughter, but much of what he does on a day-to-day basis is detached. As doers, men often think, "I do this for her, and this shows her I love her," but it may not. The moments spent together with significant words and concern is what creates the attachment or bond.

CONCERNS DADS HAVE

1. *No experience.* The concern of one dad is "We grew up boys." There's no experience in what it's like to be a girl. And even less so when there were no sisters in the home. You may be married and have daughters. If so, share this information with your husband, and if you have married sons, encourage them to learn as much as they can about their daughters.

2. *No one to talk to.* Another issue is "There's no one to talk to." This doesn't have to be a concern if there are older men around who have raised daughters, and fathering conversations could occur with them. Unfortunately, men tend not to discuss parenting with each other, leaving that to the mothers.

3. *Stereotypes.* A third difficulty is the stereotypes men struggle with. They can range from being competitive to being incompetent in the home. And a big one is the so-called "provider" role. A boy grows into a man learning that a father's role is that of a provider— and often that just translates into making money. It's easy for men to become overly involved in this area to avoid some of the inter-personal responsibility at home. This often takes away from the interaction and bonding that can only come with the daily care of children.

4. *No modeling at home.* A major hurdle for fathers is the silence of their own fathers. Most dads don't instruct their sons about being a father. Many were just lawgivers most of the time when they were there. A father of a daughter needs instruction and the freedom to be different from his own father.[2]

The Mind of a Man

What goes on in the mind of a man? What are his concerns and fears about his daughter? Many men live with a set of mixed and even contradictory responses, such as: Most fathers want to protect their daughters more than anyone else but aren't sure if they're going to be able to do it. They can be very (and overly) protective.

A father wants his daughter to be attractive and beautiful, but at the same time not have any sex appeal that will attract boys. He wants her to be married someday, but not until she's thirty. Boys need to wait to come around until she's twenty-nine-and-a-half. We're threatened by boys coming around wanting to see our daughter. We greet them with a stoic expression and a look that says, "You touch her, I break your leg." We let them know we have a beeper attached to our daughter, and we only put the shotgun down when they leave.

Fathers are concerned about their daughter's developing sexuality but they usually don't talk with their friends about these concerns.

Fathers don't understand the emotions that float through the air. As one father of three daughters said, "My home is a hormone factory. I wish they'd get in sync and all be up at one time or down at one time."

A father wants to communicate with his daughter, but since men and women (even little girls) speak different language styles it's not the easiest thing to do. There are many topics a dad would like to discuss, but often he doesn't know how to begin. Even if he is successful at starting the conversation, he's sometimes threatened by what he hears.

Fathers want to build up their daughters, but often their efforts have the opposite effect. The inconsistency of a daughter's response may put a damper on his attempts. Some dads say dealing with a daughter, especially in adolescence, is like riding a roller coaster with no seat belt!

Fathers want a special place in their daughter's life. And some days they are special. But other days they feel like the scrapings off a shoe. It's a difficult adjustment when boys take that special place that Dad used to occupy.

Conversation and humor with daughters may work one time and not the other. One moment she loves her dad's teasing, the next it's met with indignation—trying to get on the same conversational and listening wavelength is a struggle.

Fathers are proud of daughters stepping out, taking risks, and being their own person. But they're also concerned about their being too independent and not needing their dad anymore. "How do you let go of the concern?"[3]

One day a father was asked the question, "What do you want for your daughter's life?"

He thought for a moment and then said, "I want her to get the most out of life—to flourish, to discover—if not answers, then to ask good questions; to live at peace with herself and others; to be a loving and good person toward herself and others; to understand that getting along with others is a refined art that involves an understanding of human nature; their insecurities, fears, but also their dreams, aspirations, and their deepest beliefs, whether they're living them or not. I want her to be humble, gracious, and be a person of gratitude. I want others to be drawn to her because of her character qualities. But I guess these are my values. My desires. My dreams. They are what is important to this father."

He added, "One day in a conversation with my daughter, I asked her, 'What do you think a father should be?' I listened as she talked—and learned. I had spent my life talking to her and teaching her and now it was my turn to be on the receiving end.

"She said, 'I think a father is to love his daughter, be there for her, not just physically, to fix things by listening, to give advice when it's requested, to protect me when I need it, to be playful yet serious, to teach me about your life so I value your generation and its distinctives, to be consistent, to discipline but not punish, to be wise like the owl, to provide, to be trustworthy above all, to remember that you are the man who makes the strongest impression upon a daughter. What my male relationships will be like depends upon how you treat me. What you as a father will do, will be repeated over and over in my relationship with men, and just be who you are— just be yourself.'"[4]

What does or did your father want for *you,* his daughter? Has he ever expressed this directly or indirectly? Have you ever asked him? And does he know what you think a father should be? If you say yes, how have you told him? Indirectly? Directly? Calmly or in anger, verbally or in writing? Is this a discussion that would help you at this time in your life?

THE FEELINGS SELDOM SHARED

Most fathers experience an intensity of overwhelming feelings at two significant times in a daughter's life: her birth and her marriage. Listen to what most fathers never share with their daughters but really need to.

"Nothing I had imagined before had prepared me for the sight of you so perfectly made, so intent on life. Every inch of you pulsed with energy, hands groping, legs churning, and your skin glowed furnace red. I trembled. When your body convulsed for a gulp of our difficult air, I gasped. The sound of your first cry echoed through my bones. I wanted to shout. No matter how old this miracle, no matter how many times it has been repeated through the generations, it was brand new to me. You were the first baby ever born, my heart was sure of it."

Years later he told her, "Soon you'll walk down the aisle with a dancer's grace. Your hand looped through my arm, and the minister will ask, 'Who gives this bride away?' I will obey custom and your firm instructions by saying, 'I do.' Yet, I can't give you away, for you aren't mine to give. For me to claim ownership of you, as fathers sometimes out of mind have claimed ownership of their daughters, would be like a twig on a great oak pretending to have made all by itself the newest bud.

"I started out this rambling letter by recalling your birth, because a wedding is a birth of another cord. In becoming husband and wife, a man and woman do not cease to be individuals, yet they become in addition, someone new, a compound self. Two shall become one, as Jesus said."[5]

What went on in the heart and mind of your father when you were born? Do you know? Ask him . . . you might be surprised.

Three Reflections

Here are the thoughts and feelings from three other fathers. The first father wrote:

When my wife and I discovered that we were having a girl, I was not surprised. I had been coaching football for ten years at the time, and the two other coaches I had been working with had six girls between them. I thought maybe we had a shot at a boy, but now there are eight girls between us and probably nine, but we soon will see.

When Jenna was born, I remember being so tired. She was two weeks late, and my wife, Suzanne, was having a thirteen-hour labor. I was nervous, scared, overwhelmed, and excited. The doctor and nurses were great. When we could see

I WANTED TO GIVE HER THE WORLD.

Jenna's head appear, I remember feeling like I was in a tunnel. Time seemed to slow down, and I remember thinking, "I am going to protect this little girl from as much as I can." I wanted to give her the world.

I was trying to help Suzanne with breathing, and being the good coach that I thought I was, I was just irritating her. I was rubbing her and encouraging her, and she told me not to any more. So much for being a good coach!

When Jenna was finally on her way out, time stood still. I started to panic a little because she was not breathing. They cleaned her nose and mouth but she wasn't responding. They took her away from us across the room to start bagging her to start breathing. I remember thinking for a second *she may die,* and that scared the life out of me. But they quickly helped her to breathe, and I was relieved.

I was soon holding my first child. She was so little, so innocent, and I was immediately her father. Soon I would be taking her home. I had no idea how wonderful it would be to know her, teach her, play with her, and watch her grow up to be the beautiful girl that she is five years later.

She now has a little sister, Kelly, and we are going to find out soon if we will be having yet another daughter. I love my girls and find that it's amazing to watch them grow. There is a softness and gentleness that comes out when you have girls. Their hugs, their little hands in mine as we walk together. When they call out, "Daddy!" When they say, "I love you, too." When they walk me out in the morning before I go to work. When they cry in the middle of the night, and I hold them and tell them, "It's okay, Daddy is here." They are amazing and wonderful gifts from God, and I am so blessed to be their father.

The second father said:

Molly was born on December 27, a month overdue. We didn't want to lose another $1,500 by letting her arrive after January 1. Doctors had told us we would never have any children, and now we were going to have our second. I hoped it would be a girl. The doctor induced labor, and this time I was allowed to be present in the delivery room. When delivery slowed, the doctor decided to use forceps to pull Molly out. So when she was born, Molly was bruised and looked a little like a cone head. But she was beautiful and a healthy nine pounds, fourteen ounces! I cried—for joy, for not being able to keep her from being hurt, and for her mother's pain.

About twenty-two years later I was in Illinois, having just returned from ministry in Russia. I called Eve, my wife, to let her know I was safely in America. She told me that Molly had married Larry while I was in Russia and my wife was in Texas. Having already seen the movie *Father of the Bride,* I had dreamed about the intimacy of being in my daughter's wedding. I felt abandoned and betrayed. I was so numb, I couldn't cry even, though Eve was crying as she told me about it. Molly had already chosen her own path to follow, and it was markedly different from ours. In hindsight, I blame myself for not warning her about the seductive illusions our American culture offers as truth. Eve and I continue to pray for her redemption, for although she is somewhat responsive to God, she still has at least one foot planted firmly in living as she sees fit and subconsciously claims sovereignty over her life.

Meggan was born five years after Molly. No bruises, she came out looking like an angel. The doctor gave her to Eve, and Meggan immediately put her hands together as if in prayer, thanking God for getting her out of a tight place. I took pictures of her birth, and developed a slide show out of them. The last piece of music was an airy "Thank You, Lord," sung by a youth choir. I didn't cry when Meggan was born. I was too busy taking pictures. But back in the labor room where we all spent a couple of hours getting acquainted, Eve and I just kept thanking God for such a perfect gift. Meggan and I developed a special bond that was different from my relationship with Matthew and Molly. Part of this bond was around our humor. We would be laughing before her siblings and mother knew something was funny.

About twenty-four years later, I stood in the narthex of Bethany Church in Long Beach, California, waiting to walk Meggan down the aisle, then perform her wedding cere-mony, holding back tears because she was such a gorgeous bride and I was giving her away to a wonderful young man. As we walked down the aisle, I whispered to her, "You are soooo beautiful," and we both choked back tears. My tears during the ceremony were tears of closeness, of intimacy, of joy, and a few tears reminisced some of our special times together as I shared with the congregation some of her qual-ities. In the reception father-bride dance, I'll admit it now, I sobbed a couple of times, unable to hold in all the admi-ration, the joy and love I felt for Meggan. Of course, I hid the tears from everyone but Meggan.

Two months into her last pregnancy, one night, Eve went into the bathroom. Then I heard her say, "Honey, I just lost the baby." We headed for the hospital where we spent the rest of the night. The doctor confirmed Eve's mis-carriage, but "for some reason" did not do a D&C. A couple of weeks later we drove to Colorado for Christmas.

Eve suffered through a virus and strong medicine, and fell down stairs during our vacation, so when we were back home and she felt a lump in her abdomen, we were worried. Her doctor verified that she was still pregnant, and when told about Eve's miscarriage concluded that we lost one of twins. Mindy was born in July. Her first cry communicated, "Whoever's in charge can stand down now. I'm here."

Less than three months after Meggan's wedding, I began walking Mindy, who I called "My Sunshine," toward an altar we had put together in a park in Huntington Beach. She had chosen an outdoor wedding on a summer evening in an underdeveloped area of the park. A full day of cooperative hard work by everyone in our family and most of our friends had transformed the cathedral of parallel eucalyptus trees, tulle, white chairs, and fake marble pillars into a breathtaking outdoor wedding chapel. Now as we started to walk toward the altar, I softly began singing, "You are my sunshine, my only sunshine." I continued singing between partly inhibited sobs. In the ceremony I described Bryan's and Mindy's qualities and their love for each other and how God had brought them together. Their responsiveness to each other, along with memories of a mission trip to Africa with Mindy, times of laughter, learning, overcoming, and being a part of introducing Bryan to God brought tears again. As the sun set during the reception, the white twinkling Christmas lights were turned on and the atmosphere was magic. Mindy generates magic to this day in the pictures she takes and in her presence. I am still overwhelmed by the powerful feelings that accompany the memories of my daughters' births and weddings.

Here's the response of the third father:

Like most fathers, I will never forget the moment my first daughter was born. Hannah, born September 26, 1995, reached out her chubby hand and touched mine—the first hand she ever touched! I babbled like the laid-out Dad that I was! (This teary display, unfortunately, was all caught on tape.) Now, ten years later, I have three beautiful girls—including seven-year-old Kylie and two-year-old Zoe—and each birth is suspended in my mind like its own unique snowflake. Each different, each lovely.

Also, like most fathers, my hope is that my girls will grow up to be stronger, deeper, healthier, and smarter than their dad. Unlike driving a car, there is no license required to become a dad. Perhaps there should be. I know if there were, most of my friends and I would probably have had to take the test three or four times before passing!

The problem with raising my girls is that no matter how much I love them, I am flawed and will do things that leave emotional and spiritual wounds. The realization of my failures haunts me each day despite the fact that I strive to do the opposite—model Christ's love and blessing.

Remember that whatever type of father you had—good, bad, or somewhere in the middle—two things are true. First, he most likely loves (or loved) you more than you can know or more than he was able to articulate. And two, God loves you more than you can know or fully comprehend. I know—as an imperfect dad, that is where I find the same kind of grace. And only in Him will you find the perfect fatherly love you desire.

What about your father? How well do you know him? Actually, who do you know *best* in your family? Is it your mother, siblings, aunt, uncle, cousin, father? Who do you know better than your father? Who is your source of information about your dad? Who do you think your father is?

In addressing the following issues about your father, use 0 to mean "never"; 1 to mean "rarely"; 2 to mean "about half the time"; and 3 to mean "almost always/extremely."

Positive	Negative
__ Hard working	__ Underachiever
__ Confident/assured	__ Low self-esteem
__ Self-reliant	__ Dependent/needy
__ Logical/rational	__ Emotional/irrational
__ Assertive/outspoken	__ Meek/shy
__ Forgiving	__ Unforgiving
__ Nurturing	__ Cold/distant
__ Considerate	__ Inconsiderate/rude
__ Reliable/trustworthy	__ Unreliable/disloyal
__ Unselfish/generous	__ Stingy/greedy
__ Flexible	__ Rigid
__ Reflective/introspective	__ Shallow
__ Fresh/straightforward	__ Sneaky/manipulative
__ Fair/reasonable	__ Bossy/domineering
__ Accepting/understanding	__ Demanding/critical
__ Insightful/wise	__ Shallow/superficial
__ Humble	__ Arrogant/boastful
__ Open-minded	__ Intolerant/judgmental
__ Approachable	__ Intimidating
__ Religious/spiritual	__ Non-spiritual
__ Relaxed	__ Anxious/tense
__ Contented	__ Dissatisfied/bitter
__ Upbeat/optimistic	__ Depressed/pessimistic[6]

A score higher than 60 in the positive column means you have a very positive image of your father. If your score is less than 10 in the negative column, you need to ask is your view realistic? But if your positive score is less than 25 and the negative column more than 50, you have a very negative view; again, is this realistic?[7]

GETTING TO KNOW YOUR DAD

Have you ever held a "Father/Daughter" interview? It's one of the best ways to get to really know your father and build your relationship. I suggested this years ago in the book *Always Daddy's Girl*, and many daughters have used this, including my own. Sheryl lived one hundred forty miles away, and as she was going through the book she found this section. She called, and as we talked she said she read the questions, and even though we had discussed many of them, there were still some she wanted me to discuss with her so would I please call her back and we could talk about them. I laughed, realizing she wanted me to foot the phone bill; that was typical. As most fathers discover, even when a daughter leaves home and marries, Dad continues to pay some of her bills. Here are some new questions. Before you ask your father these questions, why not answer them based on what you know about your father. (By the way—be prepared—your father may ask you the same questions):

1. Do you have a favorite relative, and if so, who is or was that?
2. What are three words you would use to describe your mother and your father?
3. What's the first memory you have as a child?
4. What's the best and the worst memory you have as a child?
5. What was the first loss you experienced as a child?
6. How did your father and mother show you love?
7. What pets did you have as a child and what were their names?
8. What books did you read as a child?
9. How do you wish your mother had been different?
10. How do you wish your father had been different?
11. What was your favorite room in your home?
12. Who were your best friends as a child and as a teen?
13. What was the best Christmas gift you have ever received?
14. What was the best birthday gift you ever received?
15. Describe your first car.
16. Who was the first girl you kissed?
17. If you were in the service, how did that experience impact your life?
18. What was your first job?

19. What has been your best job?
20. What is the worst loss you've ever experienced?
21. What do I do or say that bothers you the most?
22. How did you respond to church as a child?
23. How did you respond to church as a teen?
24. If you asked God one question, what would that be?
25. What laws would you like to see changed and why?
26. Which emotions are easiest and most difficult for you to express?
27. When I cry in front of you, what goes on inside of you?
28. Whom do you miss most in life at this time?
29. What do you see me doing in ten years?
30. What do you see yourself doing in ten years?
31. What's the best advice anyone has ever given you?
32. What advice would you have for me at this time of my life?
33. What do you think about during church?
34. What piece of music speaks to you or inspires you?
35. When 9/11 occurred, can you describe what you experienced inside?
36. Whom have you lost in life that you wish you could still talk with?
37. In what areas do you see yourself successful?
38. In what areas do you wish you were more successful?
39. As a teen did you have a dream for your life?
40. How would you describe your personality?
41. What do you think heaven will be like?
42. What is the hardest subject for you to talk about with me, and what do you hope I won't ask?
43. What do you wish I had done differently as I was growing up?
44. What books have you read in the past ten years?
45. What diseases do you hope you never have to deal with?
46. What do you want people to say about you in your eulogy?
47. If you met Jesus, what would you ask Him about life?

48. Who are your closest friends today and why?
49. What was the hardest time for you being a father?
50. What do you wish you would have done differently with me, and what do you wish I would have done differently with you?
51. Describe your thoughts and feelings when I was born.
52. Describe your thoughts and feelings when I was married.

You can add other questions of your own:

1. _____
2. _____
3. _____
4. _____
5. _____
6. _____
7. _____
8. _____
9. _____
10. _____

Getting to know your father will be a process. You don't want to be an interrogator, but an interested listener. Whenever you're with your father, perhaps you could work into the conversation one question you've never asked before. Always—and I mean *always*—thank him for sharing.

Some of your questions may be answered. Others won't. You will have gaps in your understanding of your father. That's all right. All of our questions here on earth won't be answered. Just like you, your father was a work in process. And some fathers did the best they could with what they had. Your father may never be all you want him to be.

But you do have a father who *is* everything you will ever need. This is a father who planned you, made you, knows and understands you, wants you, fathers you, and will never leave you. He has engraved you on the palms of His hands (Isaiah 49:16), and He is a father to the fatherless (Psalm 68:5).

This is where every woman's hope lies, and where she can find her fulfillment—in her heavenly Father. Trust Him for whatever you need.

Postscript: To fully understand all that you have from your heavenly Father, read *He Knows Your Name* by Tommy Walker (Regal Books, 2004).

Chapter 3

MEMORIES OF DAD

Your life is filled with memories. Without memories life is incomplete. We have no past. We have a form of amnesia. In time memories fade. They lose their sharpness. We may need pictures or someone's reminder to activate them. But sometimes sights, sounds, and smells of an event can affect us more than we'd like. Those of us who have experienced a trauma such as an accident, a violent death, or abuse—maybe even seeing the towers crumbling in New York—have memories that when activated can immobilize us, creating panic or bringing back all the feelings we had when the event actually occurred.

You and I have father memories. These pictures could be a reflection of who you are today. The author of the book entitled *Father Memories* made some insightful suggestions. The father memories you have contain the emotions you had as a child. That's all right. This emotion is as important as the memory itself. When we activate memories, we must be careful not to fall into the trap of using them to blame others. It's so easy to do this.

Memory is made up of bits and pieces from what we can remember of the past. Memories are not just factual events. It's more like a collage, including feelings, images, perspectives, and fragments that we spread on a table and then piece together for our story. It becomes our life story. It is our history, and it's used to help us make sense of our lives. One woman said, "It doesn't matter who my father was; it matters who I remember he was." What would you have said about your father twenty years ago? Ten years ago? Five years ago? What would you have said about your life story twenty years ago? Ten years ago? Five years ago? You probably had different versions. There might be different themes and issues. Changes occur.[1]

One author put this in a helpful perspective:

> It is this very phenomenon that enables many reconciliations to occur. Old hurts, which seemed huge and insurmountable at one time, often recede to the back burner after a number of years as we gather new experiences in life; we frequently view the old ones from a different perspective when we are open to the changing landscape. Our lives can expand in ways that previously seemed impossible.[2]

"Time heals all wounds" is not necessarily true. Time by itself is not a healer. And depending upon what you do during that time, your pain could even increase if thoughts are fed and intensified. But when you put time together with distance and new life experiences, the intensity of some of the feelings can be blunted as well as the desire for payment. Some daughters mellow over time and want to move on, while others become bitter and stuck where they are. They allow their father to control their life and relationships even when they're seventy! It's interesting that they're angry at what he did or didn't do when they were young and how he dominated their life by this, but not letting go means you allow him to *continue* to dominate.

Dan Allender said, "Memory is to some degree a reconstruction of the past that is highly susceptible to erosion, bias and error. It is a mistake to consider one's memory completely accurate, no matter the level of emotional intensity or detail associated with the memories. We should maintain a tentative, open and non-dogmatic view toward all our memories."[3]

Some that I have worked with have said the key to understanding where they are now in life is their memories. They say their past is controlling their present life. Perhaps there is another way to look at this. If you grapple with what is occurring in your life at this time, the present, and take responsibility for it, perhaps what needs to be known about the past will become clear. One writer said, "In that sense, *the past is the servant of the present—* and change in the present clears the way for whatever God wants us to know about the past."[4]

Fathers influence us more than we'll ever know. They leave a lifelong impression upon their daughters. The author of *Father Memories* said:

> Picture fathers all around the world carving their initials into their family tree. Like a carving in the trunk of an oak, as time passes the impressions fathers make on their children grow deeper and wider. Depending upon how the tree grows, those impressions can either be ones of harmony or ones of distortion.
>
> Some fathers skillfully carve beautiful messages of love, support, solid discipline, and acceptance into the personality core of their children. Others use words and actions that cut deeply and leave emotional scars. Time may heal the wound and dull the image, but the impression can never be completely erased. The size, shape and extent of your father's imprint on your life may be large or may be small but it is undeniably there.
>
> Your father's imprint upon you is best recognized in what you remember of your father's words and actions in relationship to you as a child.[5]

From time to time it will be important to stop and take stock of what you think and feel about your father. And perhaps the question to ask is, "How did my dad affect my life?" Throughout this book you'll be asked numerous questions. Some won't affect you at all while others could activate some intense feelings. Take another piece of paper and draw a circle like the one here:

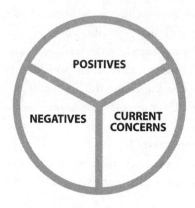

Draw and then divide it into thirds and label the sections: Positives, Negatives, and Current Concerns.

In the Positive section identify your father's positive contributions to your life and his positive qualities. In the Negative section list what you think were your dad's negatives or shortcomings. In what way wasn't he there for you? If he died, abandoned you, or you didn't know him well, what were the benefits as well as the disadvantages of his not being around? In the third area (Current Concerns) list your present-day concerns or problems with him. Write down whatever comes to mind as quickly as you can.[6]

It's better to use our memories to improve ourselves than to hate our father. Lee Ezell, who grew up with an abusive alcoholic father, said, "Yes, my dad was a poor model of a father, but I do not have to be crippled in my relationship to God the Father all of my adult life because of my earthly father. I believe my parents were responsible for what they did then; I am responsible for what I do now."[7]

EARLY RECOLLECTIONS

What's your first memory? How old were you? I've heard some amazing stories over the years, memories of people at age four, three, and even two.

Let's begin with your first memories.

My first three memories are . . .

1. _____

_____

2. _____

_____

3. _____

_____

My first memory I have of my father is . . .

_____

_____

and I was _____ years old. As I think about this I feel . . .

_____

_____

My best memory I have of my father is . . .

_____

_____

As I reflect on this memory I feel . . .

_____

_____

My worst memory I have of my father is . . .

_____

_____

As I reflect on this memory I feel . . .

_____

_____

The last memory I have of my father is . . .

_____

_____

As I reflect on this memory I feel . . .

_____

_____

Now list ten other memories that come to mind when you think about your father. Describe how these memories affect your life today.

1. _____

2. _____

3. _____

4. _____

5. _____

6. _____

7. _____

8. _____

9. _____

10. _____

What do these memories tell you about your father?

Who would you be without these memories? Memories are part of our life stories. But it's not just the memories that make up the story, it's our response to them.

Who was the source of information about your dad? True, some of it was gathered firsthand, but other people were probably involved in it as well. In fact, if Dad left you completely at an early age, or divorced your mother, the primary source of information about your father was likely your mother. What is the impact of that information upon what you believe and feel about your father? Think about what you've heard over the years from your mother. Has it strengthened your relationship with him or weakened it? What are ten comments you heard from your mother about your father?

1. _____

2. _____

3. _____

4. _____

5. _____

6. _____

7. _____

8. _____

9. _____

10. _____

Now go back and indicate which were positives and which were negatives.

RECOGNIZING ENMESHMENT

At one time were you as close to your father as your mother? How about at the present moment? I'm talking more about personal sharing than just doing things together. If you were just as close to your father as you were to her, was your mother comfortable with that? Could you call and talk to either parent on the phone without the other listening in? Could you go on a trip with either parent without the other being bothered? Some mothers want their daughter to be close to them rather than to their father. Hopefully your family of origin was healthy, and your parents cooperated rather than competed. But if there was over-involvement with one parent to the exclusion of the other, we end up with *enmeshment*.

Some daughters don't have the problem of an absent father. In their case, it's not that he's not involved in her life—he's too involved, and he won't let go. And when there is a significant degree of this in a relationship, it's called emotional incest. A daughter's sense of who she is is so limited and her need is so great to be connected to her dad that he has control over the relationship at any age. In the case of emotional incest a father uses his daughter for his own need fulfillment. You could be a daughter who wonders, "Did that happen to me? How do I know if that's what happened?"

Many wonder, since it felt normal. Can you reflect back to when you were a child? Think about it for a while. Sometimes a woman answers these questions and then asks someone else's opinion, someone who is objective and was there with you when you were a child.

Some of the difficulties a daughter might experience because of this pattern of enmeshment are illustrated by the following comments. Do any of these responses sound familiar?

"Some days I just feel worthless. Others give me love, but I don't accept it. I don't feel worthy. So what do I do? Isolate myself. I'm afraid of being rejected." Comment: This often happens because enmeshment with one parent can cause resentment in the other parent.

"Sometimes I think I can do anything. I'm really better than anyone else. I look down on others. But other days I have no regard for myself and what I'm capable of. I'm like an imposter." Comment: Self-esteem fluctuates because one minute you feel invincible and the next inadequate. When you're overly involved with a parent and are his or her favorite, you can end up with some misbeliefs about your own abilities.

"When I was a child I was around a lot of other children, but I didn't feel a part of the group. Sometimes I felt they were all better than I was, but other times I felt superior." Why does this happen? Probably because less time was spent with other children. There was some social isolation, and learning adequate social skills was lacking.

"Failure. That's the best word to describe me. I am a failure. I feel like one. What I do accomplish, which isn't much, is never good enough. I tell myself that. Others tell me. I try but never measure up." You may have compared yourself with your father, or heard from him that you weren't good enough.

"When I was growing up I felt so secure, and thought I was. There were no problems or upsets or insecurities or fear. I really didn't think so, anyway. Then I heard about denial, which is what I was living in. I walled off those problems so I could appear like I had everything under control. But underneath all that I had needs— many needs—but I didn't let them come up for air." Others rein- force this pattern by saying, "You're always on top of things" or "You always have a smile on your face." Dad saw you as very func- tional, and who would want to disappoint him? It may have been difficult to be sad or mad or afraid in front of him because of his response.

"I'm a flaming perfectionist. I admit it. I have to be. I have to succeed. Every day is tension. I can't just do my best, but I must strive for better than my best. And I never relax or let down." For many daughters, success is not an option but a necessity if you're the best, the top person. Many do succeed. (By the way, perfection- ists are wracked with guilt and anger since perfectionism doesn't work. And they often procrastinate since they won't try anything unless they're assured of success).

"Do you know who I am? If so, tell me. I don't. And I don't know what I want, either. I'd rather know what you want. I rely so much on what others say about me, think of me, or want from me." When you're too close to a parent you have a difficult time devel- oping your own sense of identity. You may have been controlled, or your father wanted you to be a replica of him.

"I hate what's going on. I'm thirty-seven going on thirteen, or so it feels. I'm an adult but I don't feel like one. If I do make a decision it's countered by my father. And most of the time I let him make the decisions. I don't want him to, but it's easier, and he bails me out financially. I like it and I hate it." Some fathers refuse to let their daughters grow up. The message stated or implied is: "You need me. You'll never make it on your own." Unfortunately, because of the lack of skill development, many tend not to make it. And some never break away, which creates a disaster when Dad dies and no one is there to pick up the pieces.

"I feel like I go in and out of other people's lives. Their problems become my problems. When they hurt, I hurt as much. Sometimes I'd like to put up a wall with a sign that says, 'Stay out.'" Some daughters end up with boundary problems as an adult. They share too much and hear too much and become too involved with others. Their time and attention is violated. But some have just the other problem—walls—no one gets close, no one gets in.[8]

Do you identify with any of these women? If so, it's time to stop and determine if you would like to change any of your responses at this time. Ask, "What is the way I'm responding doing for me? Is this positive or negative? Do my responses fit the criteria of a mature woman? If not, what do I see myself doing that would be a healthier response? What are the steps I need to take to get there?"

IMPERFECT PARENTS

All of us are flawed. There are neither perfect parents nor perfect daughters. We all have a condition called *sin*. And God loves us in spite of it. He wants us to grow spiritually, and in doing so we can become emotionally and relationally healthy. If you have set either parent on a pedestal, don't. Never idealize a parent, because it leads to disillusionment and hurt.

Hopefully your mother could see the strengths in your father and focused on these in your presence. A healthy family is one in which both mother and father build each other up, whether the other spouse is absent or present. Can you remember statements in which your mother praised your father in front of you? Did she ever criticize him in front of you? Did she ever try to get you on her side on some issue? Were there many disagreements between the two of them over disciplining you or how to raise you? Which one (if any) felt they were the expert? Who ran the house, or was it shared leadership? If your mother tried to have you become her confidante or advisor about her marriage, she was out of line. This could affect your perception of your father. Their marriage was their business, not yours.

Why should we bother with memories about our father? That's

the past, and the apostle Paul said, "Forgetting what is behind, I press on . . ." (Philippians 3:13–14). That's true. But to forget past pain we need to *make peace with our past*. What happened in our past does count. I've talked with too many who have denied the impact of their past, and this only limits their ability to heal and move forward. As your father memories unfold and are identified, life changes can occur. These memories affect the way you relate to others, how you see yourself, and even how you perceive God.

From our survey, here are some examples of how a father influenced his daughter:

He taught honesty, integrity, and a good work ethic both by word and example. He also taught us respect for all races of people and walks of life. He made me feel I could do anything or be anyone I wanted to be.

He gave me my sense of humor, my delight in little things, my optimism, my faith in God, my sense of value as a woman and as a person.

Oh, let me count the ways: He has made me practically intolerant of incompetence; he has pushed me to excel in every way, which has given me a very healthy self-image; he has taught me to work hard and succeed in the things I enjoy; he has made me believe that I "clean up pretty good"; he has made me determined to allow any children I may have to go ahead and ruin the lawn with slip-and-slide (because I could never get one lest the lawn get flattened); he has also made me determined to be proactive in helping my future kids to make special memories—a lot of my childhood was quite forgettable for me because I spent so much time with just myself and my thoughts; he has helped me to never settle for less than I deserve; he has also helped me to learn how to choose my battles; he has instilled in me that I should never expect a handout and I should work for all I get; and he has showed me (through negative example) that material things cannot make you happy.

He has been an amazing role model. He inspires me to work hard, treat people fairly, to love God, and to enjoy life. The life he made for my family is one which I hope to be able to provide for a family of my own someday. My father instilled a foundation of faith within me since I was a child that has carried me through difficult years and allowed me to become the person I am today, and to have the relationship I have with God today.

My father has had a huge impact on my faith development. He has always been the person I go to when I have a faith question, so he has contributed to my knowledge and understanding of faith/religion/the Bible, but more important, he has just been a wonderful model of our heavenly Father's love for His children. I am blessed. I have also acquired many of his personality traits——kindness to others, quirky sense of humor, generally upbeat nature. I've probably inherited some of his not so great personality traits too— taking it personally when not everyone in the world loves us, tendency to become quiet in a large group of people if the conversation becomes exclusive and we can't get a word in edgewise. All in all, he has influenced my life in a very positive way.

I honestly don't know how to answer this question. To my knowledge, he had little influence on me either positively or negatively.

Call it Oedipal or a tribute, but I married a man very much like my father. And I would do it all over again. Like my father, my husband is funny, strong, and humble—a computer-nerd, faithful churchgoer, affectionate father, and hardworking homebody. I realize psychologists have long suggested that how a girl views her father not only profoundly affects whom she will marry, but also her view of herself and of God. For many, this is a lifelong struggle. For me, it is a gift. Because of my Dad, I am a big-nosed princess who married her prince and believes in a loving God with a good sense of humor. Thanks, Dad.

I feel cheated out of the childhood I should have had. I became disillusioned with the church (my father was on the board of elders), and for a while I looked for greener pastures in what I saw as more "woman-friendly" religions. Sometimes I still have to remind myself that my father's God is not God; that I see Him through a murky film that took years to develop and will therefore take at least as long for me to scrape the crud off to see Him as He truly is.

My father was an alcoholic (we went to a Catholic church)—so now as an adult I feel sorry for him. I used to be afraid of men, and I am still rather quiet unless I am with people that I trust. I have a low self-esteem.

I definitely married someone like my father . . . hard worker, not very emotional (that's a negative and a positive), responsible, and funny. I'm thankful that he had an effect on what I see as important in a man and as a father. I had no problem trusting in God the Father at age sixteen because I had a loving and faithful and fair human father.

I have spent my whole life *not* being like him. I try to see everything as positive as possible.

From my father I learned that honesty is one of the most important character traits one can have. A good name is not to be taken lightly. He taught me the value of money—that it is to be appreciated and not wasted. One doesn't spend or live on what one doesn't have. From watching him at work, I learned that one treats everyone the same—

customer, employee, peer. If it's in your power to help some-one, do it. His form of escape was getting sick, and he often had sick headaches or stomach problems. My reaction to that has been to avoid illness until I can no longer deny it.

WHO AM I?

There are various steps you can take to change what occurred or didn't occur in the past that has brought you to where you are today. Some women have shared with me that even though they don't look like it, they feel their growth as an adult was stunted because of what happened to them as a child. Some say they feel like a child in an adult body. Many who were hurt learned to develop layers of protection. One woman said,

> I'm like a walking onion. I know it's a weird word picture, but I have all these layers of protection I wrapped myself in. That's what you find on an onion—layer upon layer of onion skin. And when I was growing up much of my energy went into making sure I was safe. But I became so safe I lost sight of who I was as a person. I'd like to "meet me," if you know what I mean, and discover who I am and who I could have been.

When I heard this last phrase it struck a chord. Many of the adult daughters I've talked with over the years have said the same thing: "I wonder who I could have been."

Here are several suggestions that can help you discover who you are, who you could have been, and what you can do now in order to move forward.

First, when is the last time you looked at photographs of your-self as a child? Find those pictures and select one or two at different ages. Choose those that really depict you at that age, and then ask yourself the following questions as you look at each picture. Some-times this could bring up intense feelings. If you can't answer the questions for a particular age, try to determine what happened at that age that is creating the blockage. Here are the questions. (Some are asked as if they are about someone else in order to help you become a more objective observer.)

1. Where were you and what were you doing?
2. How did her father respond to her at this age?
3. What was the most fun for this child at this time?
4. What kind of care and love is the child receiving at this time?
5. What kind of parenting did the child receive that was beneficial?
6. What kind of parenting did the child need that she didn't receive?
7. What kind of parenting did the child receive that was destructive?
8. What did the child learn about fathers at this age?
9. What could this child learn now that would fill in the gaps in her life and help her to feel more complete?

I WONDER WHO I COULD HAVE BEEN.

Now, having completed this for several ages, how would you *summarize* your childhood to someone else? Write a summary statement based on all the information gleaned from these questions.

If you discovered that you missed out on some things in your life at various ages, then you experienced losses. And in order to move on, it's important to grieve over those losses and eventually be able to say good-bye to them. Then you'll be able to move on with your life.

As you look at the parenting you needed but didn't receive, in what way have you received that parenting as an adult? And if you received it, did you accept it?

Martha told me her story:

I guess you could say I always wanted to please my father and hear something as basic as "good job"—but it didn't happen. I heard him say that to adults but never to me. Just once would have helped. So in my child's mind I began to think, "He said it to them, so they must deserve it. He doesn't say it to me, therefore I must not deserve it. So there's something wrong with me!" And I still want to hear that from others, and I do! Only it doesn't register. I guess I won't let it. I keep playing the old tapes, "I don't deserve it."

MESSAGES FROM THE PAST

Most of us have answering machines. We want to make sure we don't miss any messages. We pick up the phone, hear a beeping tone, dial our code, and hear the words "You have three messages." Some have call waiting and will interrupt a conversation to answer so they don't miss the message.

There are some messages, however, that some women wish would disappear. They are in their memories. They float in and out of their minds automatically, and when they invade, they disrupt their lives. The message is from the past and it's usually from their father, the first significant man in their life. Often it's even heard in their father's voice. These memories are often taken as the "Gospel truth." And there is an incredible range of them. These memory messages could include:

"You're no good."

"You're not pretty and never will be."

"You're a failure."

"You'll always be fat."

"You'll never measure up."

"No man will want you."

"You can never please anyone."

"What you feel isn't important."

"You can't trust your feelings."

"You can do anything."

"You are such a special child."

"I am so proud of you."

"You will make some man so happy."

You see how these messages vary? I wonder what messages you're carrying around—the ones that you want to keep and those you'd like to erase. Take a few minutes and reflect on your messages from the past.

Messages from Dad I want to keep:

1. _____

2. _____

3. _____

4. _____

5. _____

Messages from Dad I want to erase:

1. _____

2. _____

3. _____

4. _____

5. _____

Are you letting your father memories or messages define who you are? Too often women say, "I am who my father says I am." But which father? Your earthly father or your heavenly Father? There's a significant difference.

Some of your father messages may be labels, and they've stuck. But do they need to? Are they really true? It could be that some of these messages have been distorted by us in our remembering process. Some may be inaccurate, and what was said to us wasn't the truth. It's hard for some to admit this since a father is seen as such a powerful figure. But some fathers have lied.

Now, can you admit that you talk to yourself? It's true. We all carry on conversations with ourselves, and it's normal. It doesn't mean that you're always aware of the messages, since some have been imprinted in your mind for years. And many of our emotions are initiated and escalated by what we say to ourselves. We sometimes call this *self-talk*—these are words we tell ourselves about ourselves, our father, our mother, our spouse, and our experiences, the past, the future, and God. The more emotion that's attached to an event, the more we tend to remember. Repeated sets of self-talk over time turn into attitudes, values, and beliefs. Most come from memories. And some self-talk comes by way of pictures flashing on our mind.

Let's consider some additional messages that women have struggled with:

"You can't do anything right."

"You'll never be attractive—you won't find a man."

"You never were much good."

"Other girls would never have gotten fired like you did."

"You're fortunate you got any kind of job."

"Who do you think would want you?"

"You're a failure."

"You'll always be a failure."

"Don't plan on college. You'll never get in."

Are these friendly voices? Not at all. They're actually your enemies. They're deceitful. They distort reality. They're nothing but lies. I don't know how much stronger it could be put. If you listen to these, you'll end up with a bucket of feelings that you'd rather throw out than do anything else with them. If you listen to them, you will begin to feel worthless, depressed, humiliated, afraid, insecure, anxious, or shameful, to mention a few.

Where does all this come from? The past and our memories. Whatever happened in the past affects your response to the present. Many could even be tied to negative criticisms from their father's past. Their mistakes from the past limit your present functioning, as well as threaten your future. But you can change that, especially if you are a Christian.

Rethinking Our Messages

"Do not conform any longer to the pattern of this world, but be transformed by the renewing of your mind. Then you will be able to test and approve what God's will is—his good, pleasing and perfect will" (Romans 12:2).

Romans 12:2 teaches that we can change our living by changing our thinking. The simplest changes you can make may involve some of the labels you've attached to events in your life. *Labels can be changed*. For example, if your dad rejected you, perhaps you're saying, "That was terrible. There must be something wrong with me." You and I know what believing those statements will do to you. Reread Romans 12:2, and then challenge each part of these false statements. "It's not terrible. It's unfortunate, but not the end of the world. It's not that I'm defective. I have tremendous worth in the sight of God. It's too bad that my father didn't have the ability to recognize this." You may have to do this numerous times until this negative belief is banished.

Go back to the sample messages that many women have struggled with. If any of these (or any of your own) come to mind ask this series of questions. Let's assume your thought is "I can't do anything right."

1. Where is the evidence? What could you show to indicate this belief is true? If you were to ask three of your friends if this was true, what would they say?

2. What's another way of looking at this situation? What's an alternative response? You could make a list of what you're doing wrong, but for every one you list you need to list two things that you've done right in your life. You will be amazed at the result.

3. If your belief is true, what do you want to do to correct it? You're assuming you can't do anything right. For the next day let's assume you can't do anything *wrong*. What would that be like? One woman said, "It was ridiculous," but is that thought any more so than the other assumption (that you can't do anything right)?

Let's consider each thought and put each one in perspective:

"You can't do anything right" you could change to: "Sometimes I don't do things well, but most of the time what I do is quite good."

"You'll never be attractive—you'll never find a man." Change to: "Some days I look good and some days so-so—sort of like everyone else—and there are men who do care for me."

"You never were much good," you could change to: "I'm not perfect and never intended to be, but I have a number of positive qualities. God knows me, loves me, has sacrificed for me, and I am worth His attention. In His sight I am really somebody."

"Other girls would never have gotten fired like you did," could be changed to: "I have held other jobs in which I wasn't fired, and plenty of others have been fired. It was a good learning experience."

"You're fortunate you got any kind of job." Change to: "I am grateful for having a job, and I am qualified for a number of jobs."

"Who do you think would want you?" could be changed to: "Many people will want to spend time with me and already do. And when it comes to work, I can find a number of opportunities."

"You're a failure" could be changed to: "Mistakes are learning experiences. They create valuable lessons. I may fail at some things, but that doesn't mean I'm a failure as a person."

Do you get the idea? You're talking back to the old messages, those old lies.[9]

Some have said, "It won't work." I've seen it work. Some have said, "I can't do it." Yes, you can. You can learn, practice, and change.

Your thought life is not your own. It, like the rest of you, belongs to God. Scripture teaches that our thoughts can change. In Philippians 4:8 we are told what to think about: "Finally, brothers, whatever is true, whatever is noble, whatever is right, whatever is pure, whatever is lovely, whatever is admirable—if anything is excellent or praiseworthy—think about such things."

Remember that the power of this passage is made possible through a personal relationship with Jesus Christ. This is how the reality of peace in our lives is finally realized. In Ephesians 4:22, Paul talks about being renewed in the spirit of your minds. When you pray ask God to renew your mind. Keep track of every message from the past, challenge it, and ask God to purge your memory banks of this message. Your goal is to realize that God through the power of His Holy Spirit gives each person the ability to picture things in the way He pictures them. Every person needs a transformation of the mind in order to have the mind of Christ.

Dr. Lloyd Ogilvie, the former chaplain of the U.S. Senate, said, "Each of us needs to surrender the kingdom of our mind to God." This is an opportunity for you to change messages that are keeping you stuck.

Can your messages change? Yes. Can your life change? *Yes.*

Chapter 4

FATHERLESS DAUGHTERS

Whenever any of us goes to our doctor, we want straightforward, specific answers. We worry when we hear, "Well, I'm not quite sure. It could be this or it could be that. On the other hand . . ." Vagueness does nothing for our sense of security. Sometimes we perpetuate the problem because we can't always define the symptoms. Living with vagueness is uncomfortable. Some women are vague about their relationship with their father. They live with unrest but are uncertain whether it's connected to their father or not.

We diagnose diseases today and classify them by symptoms. It's the same in the counseling profession. We're able to give a psychological diagnosis with classification numbers based upon the symptoms. Sometimes we even have what some refer to as a *syndrome*.

Now, imagine yourself going to a doctor. He enters the examination room and asks, "What seems to be the problem?"

Your response is, "I'm not sure. I've been wounded. Sometimes I'm not even aware of it. Other times it seems to be my mind. Other times it's my heart. And then there are times when it's not really localized—it's just there, like a low-grade fever. I wish I could give you more information about my pain, like give it a name. I just feel incomplete. I have a hunger, and it's for what I needed."

This is not an isolated response. It's the voice of women whose fathers weren't there for them for one reason or another. It's the voice of the fatherless daughter.

"Where were you, Dad? I looked for you. I cried for you. I asked others where you were. And they said, 'He's right here. Don't you see him?' You were there for them, but not for me. Why, Dad, why? What did I do? What was wrong with me?"

This is the cry of a fatherless daughter—the one with the hole in her heart, crying, wounded, searching or wandering, aching inside for an accepting touch or a word from Dad. Some fathers were physically absent. Some were present but absent emotionally. Others were violators.

THE FATHERLESS DAUGHTER SYNDROME

A girl abandoned by the first man in her life feels tossed aside, unworthy or incapable of receiving a man's love. "Yes, I have love now," she thinks, "but just wait. It won't last."

Someone has said there are so many women today whose fathers weren't there for them that we have a massive choir of the wounded. Can you imagine what Father's Day means to these women?

When a woman has "missed out" on the father in her life and his influence, it doesn't stop there. How does this woman help her own daughter understand men? One woman said,

> What happens when a woman is reared and then comes into parenthood herself without the benefits of those early lessons taught by a father? She may be quite capable of transferring to her children lessons about issues related to women, but she's unable to directly translate for her children the mysteries and secrets of men. It's comparable to a blood transfusion: If you have type-A blood, you can be a donor to another person with type-A blood—but not to a person with type O. With the decline of two-parent households, the base of information and knowledge

previously developed by women about men also dimin-
ished: If we were running a blood bank we would have
declared a state of emergency and issued a call for
donors.[1]

"When no caring father's hands are available to shape his daughter, the result is as certain to emerge askew as a bowl denied the
potter's touch before it is placed in the kiln."[2]

We asked women the question, "In what way wasn't your father
there for you?" Here is what several said:

He didn't stand up to my mother, who entered a troubled
phase in my teen years, and she ended up dominating the
family and causing great instability (despite his own stability)
and scenes and trouble. Nightmare times.

My father was unplugged emotionally for a lot of my teenage years. My mom was going through a difficult time, and
my dad responded by locking himself in the garage. He
didn't want to know anything that was going on; he shut us
all out.

HE WAS NEVER THERE—PERIOD.

He was never there—period. I was raised
by my mother and grandmother.

I've never bonded with my dad. We never
had deep, meaningful conversations, and he didn't interact
with my sister or me much. I don't feel I have a very strong
relationship with my dad.

Because my mother had mental problems, my mother came
first. When she needed Dad to help her, all the focus had to
be on her. Dad was also involved in several activities outside
the family that at times I felt were selfish. I realize now as
an adult, he needed them to keep his sanity.

He was never there for me, and I finally was able to accept that he never would be when he did not even attend my baby's funeral.

He was present yet absent—the majority of my waking hours, he was outside working (in the evenings) or in bed sleeping (in the morning before school). When he was in the house for meals, there was often tension in the air. He did not attend (or, was not "present" for) school conferences, concerts, speech meets, sports events, or other extra-curricular activities other than on very rare occasions. My mom attended these events alone. If he was attending, he would not plan a schedule that would allow enough time for him to get ready. As a result he experienced stress and would move through the house angrily. He would be angry at my mom because he perceived that she was forcing a rigid schedule on him. This same situation sometimes occurred with church on Sunday mornings.

Emotionally he wasn't much of a man. I was more of a parent to him. I became aware of his weaknesses (lack of patience) and was hyper-vigilant to start the car for him on cold mornings so he wouldn't come in cussing and making our life more miserable because of his anger. He was not there for me emotionally or spiritually.

When I was young, early teens, I felt my dad never had time for me. We were very distant. I didn't feel I had a dad until my late thirties.

He was never not there for me, and I mean *never!*

Symptoms of the Fatherless Daughter Syndrome

Some believe this syndrome has symptoms as identifiable as the flu. Not everyone will experience them, but enough do to indicate these five overlapping categories need to be considered.

1. One is called the "un" factor. *Un* is used when something isn't. Years ago a popular game was called the Ungame. It was an inter-active, communicative game, yet not a game. Often a daughter with-out a father believes she is *unworthy* and *unlovable* and that's why her father left. They're sure no one would really love them. And if someone does, there's some catch to it. They believe that love needs to be earned so they'd better perform. And so if they're missing something they try to find it. In this case it's Dad's love. If he's not around, they try to find it in every man they meet.

2. Another category has two names—the abandonment syndrome, or the triple fears factor. And the presence of these can sabotage any relationship. The fears are rejection, abandonment, and commit-ment. The hurt of these is so much, why extend yourself? I've seen so many women who in subtle ways create the very scenarios they fear, which reinforces their fears. And they end up picking up the same kind of men over and over again. The author of *Longing for Dad* said, "Daddy's sudden and untimely death caused me to choose men who ultimately will abandon me, emotionally and literally."[3]

Diane Weathers, an editor for *Consumer Reports* magazine, said, "The overriding theme, of course, was fear of rejection, a dire dread that being left by my daddy had marked me for life, doomed me to eternal abandonment. Eventually I became expert at rejecting me before they found me out. I was clueless when it came to men. I felt more comfortable with types who were at best ambivalent and at worst indifferent, emotionally or physically, remote, living in another state or another country, moving in another orbit. Such men could have been dead ringers for my absent dad."[4]

Have you experienced the triple fears? And if so, to what extent? Can you identify any of the ways you may have responded with men that makes the fear come true? What are some ways you could take control of these fears and not let them interfere with your life? What are the tapes that play over and over again in your mind? For some women they are:

"I'll always be rejected because that's what men do."

"If I love someone, I'll be hurt. They'll leave me."
"I can't trust men, but I need them."
Complete the following. My other messages are:

1. _____

2. _____

3. _____

These triple fears can actually be summed up in one issue—a lack of trust. When my granddaughter burned herself on the stove, she became less likely to go back to it. What is she thinking? "It hurt me before so it will hurt me again." And so a woman says, "Dad rejected and abandoned me before. He's a man, therefore that's what you can expect from any man."

Many engage in a dance of getting close, but not too close. Some women marry but end up as married singles. She and her husband live parallel lives.

3. A third factor or symptom is the sexual healing factor. Some vacillate from being promiscuous to seeking total avoidance. Some hope that physical closeness will bring the healing they seek. The National Fatherhood Institute stated teen girls who are raised without their fathers tend to have sex sooner than those who are raised in a home with both parents. And some fatherless girls believe having a baby is the cure-all for loneliness and a preventative for abandonment. Such thinking, unfortunately, is wrong.

4. Another factor carries a different label. It's called the "over" factor. Do you know where I'm going with this? Many women overdo just about everything. They overachieve in any area they can as their message to their father: "Look at me. Look at what you're missing out on. It's your loss." Many women start climbing the ladder of success and never stop. Perfectionism creeps in, but when achieving doesn't satisfy, the next culprit can be overextension. It could be in the area of eating (or not eating), drugs, alcohol, or anything else taken to excess.

5. The final factor is RAD (Rage, Anger, Depression). Some father-less women have a caldron of anger. As one woman said, "It's like I have a volcano in my stomach. It's always there churning away, and I never know when it's going to erupt. And erupt it does."

Some women channel their father rage into obsession with drugs, food, sex, alcohol, or even success. Or the rage takes a U-turn back onto the woman and evolves into depression. Following this may be apathy, since anger hasn't worked.[5]

MOST FATHERLESS WOMEN HAVE UNRESOLVED GRIEF.

Each of these is a form of a message. Depression tells you something else is going on in your life that needs attention, and you need to listen to that message. Often depression is a symptom of grief, and most fatherless women have unresolved grief. Anger and rage are often the result of hurt. Hurt is one of those emotions we all experience but don't necessarily like to talk about. When you talk about hurt, you often relive the experience and reexperience the pain. So over time what might hurt turn into? Rage and resentment. Hurt is one of the big three uncomfortable emotions that leads to anger (the others are fear and frustration). Whenever you experience anger, look for pain. Where there is pain, something is usually broken and needs fixing.

When you're hurt, you feel vulnerable, weak, drained, hope-less, and helpless. When the pain of hurt is denied and stuffed into the subconscious, you may not think about it—but that doesn't mean it has disappeared. Out of mind doesn't mean out of memory.

What does anger do for you? It puts up a wall to protect you. And that works briefly. However, the long-term effect is that the problems you've been avoiding and trying to run from get worse. The hurt that results is always greater than it would have been if you had used your anger energy to address the original problem. The following poem illustrates what happens:

Walls of Anger, Walls of Pain

Escaping the daggers of pain that pierce my heart
I built walls of anger to protect myself from the hurt.
No one can do this to me, I claim
So I shut them all out to avoid the pain.
Lonely, empty, bitter and without joy I live.
No one can come near me, I have nothing to give.

But God has said these walls cannot stand
And so with a loving and all-knowing hand
He pushes away the bricks one by one
Until there is no protection and no place to run.

A flood rushes in and breaks over my soul,
A hurtful, healing flood that makes me whole,
For instead of a life destroyed by anger and sin,
He enables me to love, hurt, and feel joy again.
Walls of anger, walls of pain.
O, Lord, don't let me build such walls again.
　　　—Source unknown

Many fatherless women have said, "This is me. This is my story. This is my life."

It's true that women who have a good relationship with their fathers have the same issues. There can be other causes, but a fatherless daughter has an elevated risk of having these problems.[6]

- Which of the three—anger, rage, depression—do you find connected to your father?
- What are the losses you've experienced in your life associated with your father that you've never fully grieved over?

Some have referred to the problem of fatherless daughters as the hole-in-the-heart syndrome. There is that empty place. Others refer to it as a broken heart. And they do break when there's a hole where Father is supposed to be. These holes create the snowball or ripple effect that continues throughout adulthood.

73

One woman who had dated for twenty years hoping to find the right spouse said, "Have you heard of the father who was there but wasn't? It's as though he was an apparition. Like a vapor or a form that drifted through the house. One day I asked him to hold me. He looked right past me and said he couldn't—he just couldn't. I decided I would never, never ask him again."

Another woman in her forties who had dated one man after another said, "Dad was there for the first six years, and then he left. I've always wondered what he felt like—he was tall and rugged and looked like he'd be strong, in his pictures. But he never held me— never kissed, hugged, patted my head like a puppy—nothing—not even a spanking. I still struggle with this obsessive washing, like I'm not clean. As a child I thought that's why he wouldn't touch me."

Another woman said, "I've fought against growing up. I kept hoping if I stayed like a child, my father would realize what he's missed and would come back. We could start over. My two husbands kept telling me to 'grow up and get a life.' I guess that's why they said that."

Another writes of her emotionally distant father: "I'm married and I have three children. I had a father in body only. You talk about being emotionally distant. He was afraid of feelings. He was the ultimate clam. So I've got three children under the age of ten who want their needs met, and a husband who has turned out to be a replica of Dad. I knew that before the marriage, but I thought I could change him and that would prove to me that it wasn't me that was defective as a child—it was Dad, but it hasn't worked that way—so I'm still a little girl starving for attention. Where do *I* get it?"

These stories are reflective of what Elizabeth Fischel says in her book *The Men in Our Lives*:

> The daughter makes a blueprint of attitudes that affect all her choices in love, later decisions about work. In the un-tangling, lie clues to the daughter's future. Will the daughter of the absent father try to resolve her unrequited love by seeking a man in her father's image? Or will she hold herself

aloof from men, making sure she is not abandoned the way her mother was?[7]

Some hearts heal, some don't. What begins in the heart of a little girl doesn't just disappear on its own. It's there during adolescence and continues to reside in the heart of the adult woman. From all outward appearances many women look like adults, but inside there's an inner child who isn't connected to the adult. The emotional development and needs have been stunted by her father loss. And so the journey to become an adult has been interrupted by the father's departure physically or emotionally.[8]

I'm Adopted . . . Who Is My Dad?

Some daughters have a father loss because they were adopted. When you're adopted, you only have a shadow where your father was supposed to be. Even though someone else wants them, many adopted daughters (especially in their adolescence) feel as though they were damaged or discarded. Judy talked about it: "It finally dawned on me. Somebody didn't want me. Not only that, they did something about it. They gave me away like I was a discard to the Salvation Army furniture store. I understand Mom doing it. She was sixteen. But he never stayed around for my birth. I've come to grips with it. It's not my loss. It's his."

Many daughters have a distorted view of men because they feel like a discard. This is a major loss for a woman, what we call an *ambiguous loss*. Dad is still alive in his daughter's mind, and even her heart, but he's gone physically. Missing in action. Some search for years feeding on bits and pieces of information. But there's never any assurance they'll find him. It's hard to find any closure with an ambiguous loss. Even if they find him, he's not Father. He never was. He's a stranger.[9]

If you were adopted, answer the following:

- When the question "Who was your father?" is asked, who comes to mind?
- If it's not your birth father, what are the reasons?

- How did you learn of your birth father? How would you describe him?
- When was the first and last time you saw him?
- How have you experienced for yourself his not being in your life?

SEARCHING FOR DAD

When a father is absent for any reason, there is still a strong connection between father and daughter. Daughters search for their fathers or for a substitute—even numerous substitutes. There are so many stories about daughters who went on a quest for their father with disastrous results. Who doesn't know about the life of Marilyn Monroe, who was abandoned by her father before birth? She searched all her life for substitutes—look at the powerful, protective men she went after: The sports hero Joe DiMaggio, playwright Arthur Miller, actors, President John F. Kennedy, Attorney General Robert Kennedy. It didn't matter whether they were married or not. Arthur Miller appeared to be a perfect father. He was older, successful, dignified, assisted her with her education, and introduced her to a high level of society. But she sabotaged the marriage by her moods and affairs so he too abandoned her. She then went into affairs with the Kennedy men, who weren't about to legitimize their involvement with her. Marilyn, the abandoned daughter, continued to be involved with men who repeated the abandonment. Some call this the *repetition compulsion*. Her choices of men never satisfied her longings, never lasted, and in the end her father was never found. Her life ended tragically.

Playwright Eugene O'Neill left his family, which included three daughters. The few times he saw one of them, Oona, before she was a teenager, were unpleasant and unloving. She always heard about him, since his name seemed to always be on Broadway. And because of who he was, Oona was accepted into New York society. She was very attractive, and at eighteen she married the famous actor Charlie Chaplin. He was fifty-three. And the marriage worked. They appeared happy, had eight children, and were married thirty-four years. They seemed to be inseparable.

Oona's father and husband were very similar. Both were raised in show business families by mentally disturbed mothers and alcoholic fathers. Both of their fathers were known to be moody, domineering, egotistical, and had several failed marriages. And both were at the height of success in the theatrical world. Charlie Chaplin adored her, and Oona found her father substitute in him. But they were too close. She never became an independent woman. When her husband died, it was as though she died also. She was too dependent on him and spent the rest of her life in seclusion. Once again she was abandoned.[10]

The words, "Daddy, I've been waiting for you" are said in many contexts. It's the little girl in the mall who wandered away from her father while on a shopping outing. After two frantic hours of searching every one of the fifty stores, using security guards and police, the frantic father found his daughter sitting on a chair in the store where she began her wanderings. Her father cried out, "Where have you been?" Her response was "Daddy, I've been here waiting for you."

A ten-year-old looks up to the stands where all the parents and others are sitting and watching the soccer game. There's an empty seat next to her mother, where her father was supposed to be sitting. Sound familiar? The promise to be there at the ballet or piano recital, the orchestra concert, the parent-teacher conference, the birthday party, or one of a hundred different events—an empty place because of a delayed father or a forgotten promise. When he arrives late or at home after the event is long over, his daughter sees him and says, "Daddy, I was waiting for you."

Many adult daughters have been saying this for years. It could be for the father who has totally disappeared, or the one who keeps promising to get together but never does, or the one who only shows the hard, controlling, high expectation, critical side of who he is, or it could be the father who is there but then again he really isn't . . . for each and every one a daughter could say, "Daddy, I've been waiting for you." She might wait year after year, hoping that Dad will walk into her life physically and emotionally and say, "I am here for you. You don't have to long for me or want anymore." Is this what you are saying?

Daddy might come, but it takes time. His moving into your life could be a slow, gradual process. It will take adjustment. But then again, the door may always remain closed, and your father may never return. Your waiting will need to be relinquished for your sake. And it can be.

There is another option available to you, whether your father returns or not. There is one you could say this to and have a guaranteed response. To God, your heavenly Father, you could say, "Daddy, I've been waiting for you," and the words of acceptance you will hear are "I'm so glad, because I've been waiting for you for a long time!"

Chapter 5

DAUGHTERS OF DIVORCE

My relationship with my father was more or less like a checkbook. My parents have been divorced since I was three. He has lived in another state my whole life. I grew up on airplanes, going to visit him for two weeks every summer. I was always a part of his life, but he was never a part of mine. As I grew older I started demanding that he come visit me. We have grown closer through the years because he has chosen to be a part of my life now.

My parents were divorced when I was in kindergarten, so I had very minimal contact over the years with my alcoholic father. When we did go visit him, we were visiting his wife, because he would be out working, or out in his garage working on his antique cars. I was very close with my stepfather and have regretted not having him give me away at my wedding instead of my dad.

Relationships are the fabric of our life. We feel like a whole person when all the pieces are in their proper place. Sometimes there are small rips in the family fabric, but they're patched or sewn up and you go on. But when a significant member of the family isn't there, or isn't who they should be, the entire fabric of the family is torn, often from top to bottom. Mother and Father are significant members. The empty place in our life can be carried for years. One woman said, "The distance between my father and me was the worst experience of my life. It was like an abscessed tooth that would not go away but continually throbbed."

Many daughters have grown up divorced. When a mother and father divorce, the children are divorced as well. It doesn't improve their lives—it has just the opposite effect. And the effects are *not* temporary. They shape lives. Abandonment by divorce puts unique pressure upon a daughter, especially if Dad is still in the picture. The result—divided loyalties—may be on the child's part or the parents, if they foster the competition.

How does divorce affect a preschool daughter? Many of the women whose parents divorced when they were this young say that what they fear the most as a result of their experience is intimacy. Commitments seem risky, as they live with fears of abandonment, humiliation, and rejection. These issues are carried with them for years.

If you were a daughter of divorce, your feelings may vary. There was fear and confusion, but if there was continual fighting between your parents, you probably also experienced some relief. Some children experience a sense of numbness to ease their pain. They're confused over whom to really live with, and become even more confused when one or both parents immediately connect with another partner. Adolescent girls fluctuate between anger and numbness. The latter was their way of coping with the years of turmoil prior to the divorce. But often their school life and social life is disrupted during a time when they're trying to figure out just who they are. Their ability to trust is shattered, since the most significant adult in their life has let them down. That hurts, and anger often follows.

There's one other factor that is rarely considered—how divorce affects the father. Consider these factors:

When the gravity of occasional parenting finally hits a father, it's like getting broadsided from a blind spot. Constantly playing hello/good-bye, feeling more grief than they bargained for, dealing with anxious, demanding, and sometimes hurt and surly kids, these fathers privately begin to wonder if their children really miss or even need them in their life. The typical non-custodial pattern—every other weekend and an additional few hours on a weekday, some holidays and maybe a month in the summer—is hopelessly inadequate in terms of preserving a close relationship with another human being, especially one who happens to be growing and maturing at a dizzying rate. And so fathers drift further and further out of the loop. God forbid that anything untoward should happen between a non-custodial father and his child because it will take a month to work out a twenty-minute understanding even with an average, mulish kid.[1]

If your parents were divorced, how did this impact your father? Have you asked?

CHARACTERISTICS OF ACOD

There's a term and a label now that you're an adult—ACOD—Adult Children of Divorce. As an adult daughter you may wonder why you are the way you are and why you do what you do. The following are the most common characteristics of an adult child of divorce.

1. *"Little Adult."* A daughter of divorce can become very proficient in taking responsibility, but usually more for others than for herself. It's often overdeveloped. With parents emotionally unavailable, some older daughters begin to parent their younger siblings or even their parents. Some have been called "little adults" since as a child they took on adult roles and in the process put some of their developmental needs on hold. This leads to reacting in adulthood as a child. Often a daughter of divorce has difficulty defining who she is. The sense of self doesn't develop. This is what happens when our efforts go exclusively into helping others. Have you ever asked, "Who am I, really?"

What can you do? Learn about yourself and how valued you are in the eyes of God. Read this passage several times a day: "Long ago, even before he made the world, God chose us to be his very own through what Christ would do for us; he decided then to make us holy in his eyes, without a single fault—we who stand before him covered with his love. His unchanging plan has always been to adopt us into his own family by sending Jesus Christ to die for us.. And he did this because he wanted to!" (Ephesians 1:4–5 TLB).

Evaluate your excessive doing for others. It's all right to say no. Become aware of what you're thinking and feeling.

2. Control Needs. Another characteristic found in ACOD is attempting to control everything. Divorce leaves you with control needs. It also changes the pattern of relationships. You feel like if you have control you can keep further bad things from happening. And it is especially important to you to control relationships. But be aware that control can move into rigidity. Control is a good way not to feel your own feelings. It actually gives people less of what they're after.

What can you do? Just the opposite. You're not in control and never will be. It's an illusion. Give yourself and others *freedom*. Begin to depend upon God and let Him make decisions in your life. An excellent book to read is *Control Freaks* by Les Parrot (Zondervan).

3. Fear of Conflict. Many adult daughters struggle with another characteristic—the fear of conflict. Usually conflict is at the heart of a divorce, and often it is angry, even violent. So the memories of conflict are not positive. It wasn't safe emotionally, and perhaps not physically. Boundaries were violated, and as a result some children were traumatized. Some daughters are very adept and intuitive about any pending conflict and are quite skillful in people-pleasing. They're so good they even seem to be able to read others' minds.

Sometimes the custodial parent will perpetuate conflict between themselves and their child. In some divorcing homes the conflict is "out in the open," while in others it's constantly rumbling underneath the surface like a volcano ready to erupt. It's quite easy to transfer the meaning of your family's conflict to current relationships, including marriage. If conflict equaled divorce, you could interpret every current conflict as the beginning of a breakup. Sometimes it's easy to confuse closeness or intimacy with conflict. You fight and then you make up. You fight and make up again and again. For some it was the only way to make contact with their parents. Many women are afraid of conflict, but they still use it because it's what they learned by watching their parents.

What can you do? Have you learned good communication skills in order to resolve differences? If there is a problem, use simple skills such as asking, "What is the real issue here?" "What is my contribution to it?" and "What do I want, and what do you want?" If conflict is ongoing and intense, find a safe place and a safe person. Don't withdraw from differences but find healthy and calm ways of resolving them. If anger is a problem in any way, read Oliver and Wright, *A Woman's Forbidden Emotion: How to Own, Express, and Use Your Anger to Grow More Spiritually and Relationally Alive* (Regal Books, 2005).

4. Need to Take Sides. Daughters of divorce tend to take sides, and why not? What do you learn when parents divorce? That's right. Who's to blame? Who's at fault? It's one way to make sense of what's occurring if you are placed in the messenger role: "Tell your father . . ." or "Tell your mother . . ." This role is unhealthy and uncomfortable for children. You grow up too fast. Parents sometimes manipulate to get you to collaborate. Sometimes you even end up spying. And so you wonder why side-taking is a part of your life as an adult.

WASN'T I
WORTH
LOVING?

―――――――

What can you do? Just step out of side-taking. Watch how you might get hooked into it. If your father or mother pushes you for information about the other parent, respond with "You'll need to ask [him/her] yourself." At first it may feel uncomfortable, but eventually it will feel comfortable. Remember, when you take sides you: (a) don't have all the facts; (b) have information that has been slanted; (c) are putting yourself in the position of a judge. Look for the truth. Let others know you're for both parties and won't be taking sides. This can occur even as an adult.

5. *Feelings of Abandonment.* An ACOD daughter feels abandoned. This is a common theme addressed in this book. It is a main issue ACOD face. In a divorce, adult needs take priority over a child's needs. Caretakers aren't as available, life is disrupted, and losses increase, but they often aren't identified as losses. Yes, there's often physical as well as emotional abandonment. A child could be indulged with material goods, but these don't make up for the loss. You may feel alone even when you're with others. You feel unworthy to be loved, and you fear being left on your own. The plaguing question floating through the minds of children of divorce is: "Wasn't I worth loving?"

The irony of the problem is that you learned so much about abandonment that you may even abandon yourself. How? Many daughters aren't even aware of their own needs or feelings and set them aside in order to stay in control. There's one other behavior that's common: To prevent being abandoned again in a relationship, it's safer to abandon the other person first. Do any of these characteristics sound familiar?

What can you do? Begin to look at who you are and what your needs are. What are you doing for yourself? Don't assume others will abandon you. Sometimes women behave in ways that lead the other person to abandon them. Do you ever leave yourself emotionally? Take time for yourself each day for prayer, Bible reading, and reading devotional books for women. Make a list of those who have stuck by you and haven't abandoned you. Identify the way this fear has been determining your responses to others and develop healthier responses.

6. *Difficulty Setting Boundaries.* This characteristic should be no surprise. ACOD have difficulty setting limits and personal boundaries. Parents' expectations violated your boundaries, and in trying to appease everyone, you didn't learn how to say no to anyone. This pattern can follow you into your own marriage or work situation. Others are allowed into your space. It's easy to jump into relationships too soon. Letting others invade your life, and then behaving without limits, damages your self-esteem and soon leads to depression.

What can you do? When asked for something, or to do something for others that you feel is out of bounds, there are two responses you can choose from: *No* or *I'll think about it and let you know.* The fear of others not liking you or becoming upset when you don't comply can undermine your resolve. Try this: Don't assume the worst. Why do you need others' approval? Delay commitments. Respect others' boundaries. And be sure to read Henry Cloud and John Townsend, *Boundaries* (Zondervan, 1992). There are several editions available, including a workbook and *Boundaries With Kids*, and the information has changed many lives.

7. *Feeling Helpless.* Have you ever felt helpless? It's another characteristic of ACOD. And there's a very good reason. A thirty-year-old woman said,

> I still have these recurring dreams. It's obvious why. It's what I thought as a child, and even now feel the same. I wasn't able to stop the divorce. I pleaded. I cried. I yelled. I prayed. But there was nothing I could do to stop them from divorcing. I knew if Dad left I wouldn't see him enough. Oh, he promised, but the visits diminished. I was

so mad. One week I'd be so helpful and responsible, and the next week I was a brat.

If a daughter couldn't help her parents stay together before, what does she do now? Sometimes she overprepares; other times she feels immobilized and becomes passive. Sometimes a divorced child is hindered from learning good communication and relational skills. You may even hesitate to ask for what you want, assuming that your request will be rejected.

What can you do? Identify when and why you feel helpless. If you're not sure how to respond, look for other suggestions. Communication skills can be learned from books, seminars, and special education classes. If you feel paralyzed and unable to act, identify the fear in what you're saying to yourself at the time. It could be that the situation reminds you of what happened in the past. Remind yourself that you can be different now. Spend time imagining how you would like to respond and rehearse that in your mind rather than your past responses.

8. Idealizing or Blaming Your Parents. This characteristic is one that is common to many children, not only ACOD. But here it occurs because of the experience of divorce. You either idealize or blame one or both of your parents and then transfer those feelings to other authority figures. And the majority end up feeling especially estranged from Dad. The reasons are many and varied. Children can have a hard time understanding why their father left them financially impoverished. Often the time they did have together with him was superficial—doing "activities" together. Dad wasn't available emotionally. Because of the absence of unconditional love and acceptance, children look to other authority figures to fill these needs. But in most cases they either don't receive what they need, or they become slaves to finding it for the rest of their lives.

The tension created in a child by divorce is intense. One parent may be idealized while the other is blamed. Often in a few years this flip flops. The problem with either response (idealizing or blaming) is that it's all or nothing. Neither enables the child to see the positive along with the negative. The worst part of idealizing a parent is that the child is forced to live with a fantasy. Real trust can't be built.

So what can you do? Begin by listing the fantasies you have about your father. How have you idealized him? What do you blame him for? Now go back to your lists and think of other possibilities for each statement. If you have difficulty with this, share your list with others who are knowledgeable about your father. They may have a different slant on what happened. Have you ever discussed the divorce with each parent separately on an adult-to-adult basis? Illusions need to be turned into truth, and often there are surprises in store for you.

9. *Unrealistic Expectations for Relationships.* Finally, and unfortunately, those who are children of divorce have unrealistic expectations for their relationships and marriages. It's right not to want to repeat what went on in their childhood home, but unless they take *corrective action*, there will likely be several problems.

How can you have *normal* relationships, intimacy, and family dynamics if you have to guess at what they are? There's no real model to follow for ACOD. Reality is what you've experienced. You saw aggression—quarrels, manipulation, and violation of boundaries. You might know something is wrong about all that but not know another way of relating. You know relationships could be risky, so why try to form them? And when they marry themselves, ACOD aren't sure what to do. Some say, "It has to last." Others say, "If I don't like it, I'll divorce and get out. I won't be miserable." Too many women look to their husband and marriage to be everything their parents' experience wasn't. But we have to remember that *perfect* husbands and marriages don't exist. Even a good marriage won't make up for an unpleasant childhood. Marriage

REALITY IS WHAT YOU'VE EXPERIENCED.

and commitment aren't solutions, but rather new opportunities where growth can occur.

What can you do now? Grow and learn as much as you can. Have realistic expectations. Read all you can, complete premarital counseling before you marry, look for an ACOD support group or general counseling. Help is available![2]

If you wonder who you are and why you do what you do, there are reasons. Go back over the nine characteristics discussed above. Which of these are true for you? What can you do next to move on with your life?

Perhaps you're like many women who grew up with divorced parents. You feel you were deserted by one or both of them. It's the way many women feel about their fathers, whether it was a real desertion or not. There are times when a daughter feels forsaken, abandoned, and so alone she can't see the presence of anyone else around her—even God himself. An unusual feeling? No. David was there. Sometimes he felt God had abandoned him. But he also said, "If my father . . . should desert me, you [Lord] will take care of me" (Psalm 27:10 CEV).

The feeling of being forsaken is one of the most painful feelings we can experience. It's the ultimate rejection. Jesus cried out on the cross, "'My God, my God, why have you forsaken me?'" (Matthew 27:46). But we also have these words: "Never will I leave you; never will I forsake you" (Hebrews 13:5). Expect that some people in your life will forsake you. Perhaps your dad did in some way. People are flawed. We all are. But also expect that God will never forsake you—because He won't. He's God, and He is always loving and faithful; He never forsakes those who trust Him. Thank God for that.

Chapter 6

MY DAD DIED

The death of a parent at any time is a major loss to a child. It changes your life in so many ways and brings with it the loss of certain hopes and dreams. It can be not only the death of part of your past but part of the present and future as well. If your past with your father was lacking, you may have been looking forward to a new future with him. But now that is gone. Perhaps you had a list of questions to ask, or grievances to share, or a confrontation that you had waited years to express. That opportunity is lost along with your father.

Your identity undergoes a change, and in a way you feel orphaned. Your sense of loss is affected by your father's spiritual condition as well—whether he was a believer or not. If your father died at a young age, you also mourn the opportunities you feel he lost, the years he would never live, and the dreams he would never fulfill. His death can lead you to question what his life was for and what it meant.

If you had cut yourself off from your father before his death, you could be affected differently than if you were still talking. If your separation from Dad was one of avoidance because of your differences, your grief experience could contain guilt and uncertainty about what transpired between the two of you. For some there may be a feeling of relief as part of your grief. If you experienced a mixture of feelings for your father, including rage and a desire for him to be punished, along with the sense of loss, you're not alone. Relief is the feeling that most don't share with others. If their fathers were unrepentant abusers, daughters may finally feel safe when death takes away that threat. This is what happened to a good friend of mine, Carolyn. Here is part of her story:

Carolyn Koons had long been estranged from her father, who had threatened to kill her when she was a child. She had eventually run away from home. The crisis came in 1977, when a campus operator at Azusa Pacific University, where Carolyn teaches, relayed a message to her: "Tell Carolyn that her dad called and that I'm on my way, and this time it's for good."

As Carolyn fled for the safety of her home, she asked herself: *Why am I still running from my father's anger, and why is he still haunting me? It seems so senseless. His hatred for me has already ruined his life. Why is he so intent on ending mine? I walked out of his life years ago. I let go. Why wouldn't he? Why couldn't he just leave me alone? He's terrorized all but the last fifteen years of my life. This time he is finally going to kill me.*

Clifford Arthur Koons had a stroke while driving across Los Angeles to the Azusa Pacific University campus. Carolyn was surprised when her brother, also named Clifford, called her: "I've got news for you." His voice changed, and I sensed him groping for words, so I waited. "Dad died last night."

"What?" His words shot right through me. Somehow, without really thinking it through, I had always imagined my dad would outlive me.

"The hospital called last night. He died of alcoholic poisoning."

There was silence over the phone lines as the pronouncement sank in. I didn't feel anything at all. He'd been there—violent and mean—every single day of my life. How could he and his threats just disappear, vanish like that?

Finally the silence seemed too long, and I wanted to clear
the confusion in my spirit. "Clifford, what do you feel?" I
asked softly.

With a sigh he gathered his thoughts. "Nothing."

"Neither do I," I admitted. A whole life lived, millions
of words and emotions communicated, pain and destruction
strewn all along the way, and at the end all we who knew
him could feel was nothing?

Carolyn Koons tried to put the death into perspective:
Lord . . . I looked up to heaven. *Does this mean it's really over?
Does this finally release me from the gun that has been pointing at
my core for all these years? You mean I don't have to spend the rest
of my life looking over my shoulder and wondering if my dad is just
a few paces behind me? It really is over, God?*[1]

Unspeakable Loss

If you were quite young when your father died, you were in
every sense at a loss for words—even if you had a vocabulary to talk
about losing Dad. The flood of feelings that you had at that time and
couldn't understand was so powerful it probably overwhelmed any
of your thinking abilities that did exist at that time. You didn't have
any organizing framework in which to put the loss.[2]

You see, you didn't have the language to even try to make sense
of your father's death. And his death took away your belief that the
world was a safe place. If your home consisted of you, your mother,
and your father, then half of the significant people in your life were
gone. And that could leave you wondering if the other parent might
not leave as well. One daughter said, "It was like a dark cloud
descended into my world, and there weren't words strong enough
to blow it away. I'll never forget the day my world changed, and it
changed forever. I divided time from that point on as *before* Daddy
died and *after* Daddy died."

Another daughter said, "I was ten when my father died. After
he died I became a little adult."

Hear the pain in the following account: "Dad's death taught
me not to trust life. What I believed in was swept away. How bad

did it affect me? I live in California and I'm used to earthquakes. They're always measured on a Richter scale. Everyone says if we ever have an 8 on the scale, California will be gone. Dad's death felt like an 8."

Another said,

LIFE

CHEATED   When my father died, it's like something
                was ripped out of me that was irreplace-
    ME.   able. It's as if we're all made up of a series
    ____   of building blocks that mount over time,
                new experiences with families and
friends—when someone dies it's like ripping out your foundation. Something is missing but it can't be replaced. It's
always missing. Without him my future was empty—no
longer safe or hopeful, just empty. I became emotionally
distant. And I was angry. I was cheated. He cheated me.
God cheated me. Life cheated me. A daughter shouldn't
have to grow up without her father.[3]

You're probably aware of the multitude of feelings a child experiences at a father's death, and yet one of the most common feelings is shame. It comes about from several sources. For a child, just being associated with death can be shameful. It's embarrassing. If you're called out of class at school, it's embarrassing. And you're embarrassed if you cry. One of the worst deaths for a child is the suicide of a parent.[4]

If you were an infant when your father died, and there was no stepfather, then someone who loved you was torn away from you. You only knew *absence* and possibly weren't sure what you were missing until you saw other little girls with their fathers. And it's not only absence, but the additional loss of seeing what a father was to do. If there were older siblings, you heard them talk about loss, but it may not have made sense to you. The others had memories and you had none. When you looked at your father's picture, you had a different response than your siblings. And if you married and had children, you weren't sure of your husband's father role.

The early death of a father robs a daughter of memories. As a result, she sometimes makes up her own memories, which often idealize her father. Daughters who lose their fathers to early death are frozen in time. They had no chance to see their father grow and change or display weaknesses and strengths. In other words, they didn't see their father as a real person. So they may have invented in their mind the father they wanted to have.

We expect older adults to die, especially after their children are raised and grandchildren or great-grandchildren begin to appear. But death at any age is always an unwelcome intruder. If death took your father early, it happened "out of order," which disrupted what you believed about your world. It was no longer secure or predictable. You thought you could understand it, and you couldn't.

Here is how one woman described the effect of her father's death:

When I became a Christian, my connection and prayers were very narrowly focused on Jesus. He was my Savior, my friend, my companion. He loved me, took away my fears, and gave me the confidence that I could face life and its many complexities. For a long time I had no sense of who God was, and I accepted the truth that He was our heavenly Father who loved us so much that He sent His own Son to die for my own sins. I usually started my prayers with "Dear Heavenly Father," but it was Jesus who was in my mind as I prayed, and it was Him I prayed to.

I also struggled with the question of why God let my father die. My mother and father met when they were both thirty-four, married at thirty-five, and my brother, their first child, was born when they were thirty-six. They had me when they were forty, and my father died at forty-two. My mother was madly in love with him, and I don't think she ever fully recovered from her loss. I think she bounced between depression and hope. I sensed it was very hard for her to carry the responsibility of providing our support, and she had little time to spend with us. It was my grandmother that I bonded with and who was most like a mother. I don't think I was angry at God, but the question of why He let him die was frequently on my mind.

The answer didn't come until a few years ago. I met Jane at my computer class, and we became good friends. Sometimes I think I played the role of surrogate mother. She would pour her heart out to me about her rage against her father, who beat her regularly, and her mom who never tried to stop him. He was big, probably weighing more than two hundred fifty pounds, and she is only five-foot-two. One time he threw her across the room, and her hip broke the screen on the TV. Frequently he would push her against the wall with his hands around her throat, and she thought he would kill her. As soon as she graduated she left home and eventually found her way to Southern California, living first in the Hollywood area and then came to Orange County. It dawned on me one day that there were far worse things than not having a father. I also met a man who had a similar history with a stepfather, and he too left home after graduation. His abuse was not as violent but it has scarred him. He would like to have someone as a friend and spouse but is afraid to trust out of fear of betrayal and hurt.

For the first ten years of my life I lived in an extended family. My uncle and grandfather were the two father figures in my life. I basically filled the void of my father with someone else [uncle and grandfather] and looked at couples and men that I admired and considered the qualities I saw. Because my brother was abusive verbally and hit me a lot, I learned to look beyond a super good-looking guy [like my brother] and looked for kindness, unselfishness, loyalty, a sense of humor, and other good characteristics.

The things I missed were: sitting on Daddy's lap, having him read stories to me, and hearing him say how pretty I looked when I dressed up for a date. I also missed things that were male: a man's whiskers and their scratchy feeling, to be able to freely touch a hairy chest and feel his muscles, to be close enough to smell his after-shave lotion, to be able to roughhouse with him knowing he wouldn't hurt me, and to have someone strong and sure to stand beside me and protect me from the fears and difficulties of the world. I saw many of these things between my husband and our girls.

My father was born to British aristocracy and grew up with servants. Mom did say once that he expected her to do everything a wife would do plus the extras a servant would do. She was raised in the southern tradition of being a feminine woman first. My recent insights have led me to believe that I might well have grown up in a home with a stormy marriage and terrible fights between my parents, and possibly even divorce. My father seemed to have faith in God and grew up in an Anglican church. Neither had a personal relationship with the Lord.

It was my loneliness and need for love that drove me to Christ, and in a very complete way my life changed forever. I have seen my brother, my niece, my aunt, and my mother turn to God with real faith in salvation through Jesus and His forgiveness. Because of my faith and the power of prayer, my loved ones won't be separated from God but will walk in His love.

HIS CONTINUING PRESENCE

The famous tennis pro Arthur Ashe concludes his autobiography with a very moving letter to his daughter, Camera. Ashe knows that he is dying as he writes the letter and knows that he will not live to see his daughter grow into a woman. His letter is filled with fatherly advice, advice he knows he will not be able to give her in person. Nonetheless, he wants to pass on to his only child his experience and his wisdom about the world. He gives her very practical advice about how to manage her money, how to respect her growing sexuality, how to understand issues of racism and sexism, and how to respect the roles that family, education, and sports play in the life of an individual.

He concludes his letter:

I may not be walking with you all the way, or even much of the way, as I walk with you now. Don't be angry with me if I am not there in person, alive and well, when you need me. I would like nothing more than to be with you always. Do not feel sorry for me if I am gone. When we were together, I loved you deeply and you gave me so much happiness. I can never repay you, Camera. Wherever I am when you feel sick at heart and weary of life, or when you stumble and fall and don't know if you can get up again, think of me. I will be searching and smiling and cheering you on.

In his last months of life, Ashe remained a caretaking parent for his daughter. His final thoughts were how he could continue to be a presence in her life even after death had taken him away.[5]

Whether a father is there or not, he is a presence, as Elyse Wakerman describes in her book:

Most women have a man that got away, a man that they have loved and lost. For us that man was Father. The first man that we had ever loved. With his presence, he had introduced us to the delight of being the female recipient of male love. With his disappearance, he had taught us the precariousness of love. Whether he died or abandoned us, we felt rejected. Despite, perhaps because of, this betrayal, he remained an indomitable force within us, an idealized standard against which all else would be measured, and found wanting. The man that got away was a constant presence in our private worlds; yet it was comforting, now that we could speak of it, to find others there.[6]

Heiress Gloria Vanderbilt, whose father died when she was an infant, used to play a game in which she imagined that her father had left behind an important letter just for her: "My favorite [game] was that he had written me a letter, a really long one, and hidden it in some secret place for me to find. Maybe, even, there would be a knock on the door, and standing outside, there would be the postman with a letter, special delivery, addressed to me, from Guess Who."[7] Vanderbilt's fantasy is a poignant example of a child's need to invent a connection with a parent she never knew. Because the fantasies of the connection to the lost parent grow in a field marked by absence, they often reveal what was missing in the child's life. These are fantasies of a longed-for but never known connection.[8]

Another woman who lost her father when she was six is now a social worker and conducts grief recovery groups for adults whose parents have died. Because of her firsthand experience she can truly care for others and understand their loss. She said, "For a very long time, I believed that the only major thing that ever happened in our family was my father's death. It influenced what I did, it excused what I couldn't do. Everything else seemed to be viewed through the loss of that event."[9]

"My father died of cancer when I was eight years old, leaving my mother at the age of twenty-nine with two children, several years of college education, little money, and few marketable skills. No doubt my lifelong professional interest in helping children, especially those suffering loss and separation, has its roots in my own continued mourning for my father and in my compassion for my mother's gallant struggles to protect my younger brother and me from the economic and personal hardships that she faced daily."[10]

Another older daughter said, "Because my father was dead I was different as a six-year-old. It said something about my value as a person. I felt branded, like I wasn't just different from others but less than. I wanted to hide this from others so I would have value. I missed out on something protective and reassuring. I now realize that Daddy's death was not just an isolated event in my childhood. It was something that happened that affected everything I did, I was, and would be."

RECURRING TIMES OF GRIEF

Sometimes it's not the death of the father that is so devastating but the way the news is conveyed to the child and the mother's response. Some daughters are simply told he's gone away or on a trip. Some are told not to cry, and they learn to stuff their feelings from then on. If a daughter could see her mother burst into tears and openly grieve, it would do her so much good and free her up to weep as well. Too many mothers hide what shouldn't be hidden. If information isn't given to the daughter, she will make it up since she's the only one she has to talk with. Sometimes the scenarios in the child's mind are quite morbid—she may become convinced that everyone important in her life may die as well. Some daughters are haunted by this fear of abandonment by death. And what does she do with all her childhood grief?

For many women the sadness they carry about in adulthood could be traced to childhood loss. With children, their limited capability to process a death cognitively as well as grieve properly means they usually re-grieve at major developmental times of their lives. And the loss can come back with intensity. It could hit at a graduation; first date; prom; turning sixteen, eighteen, or twenty-one; when she marries; when she has a child. And it's not just that he died . . . he *left* them. And that's what really hurts. One woman wrote this poem:

And you asked where he went
And they said:
Heaven.
And they took you to a field of tombstones and Columbine.
They said
This is where his perfect body lay.
And you were confused.
Now there was two of him
And none of you.

Another said,

I never knew my father. At times I wondered if I ever had one. I never saw him. He was a dimensional face on a photo. In some ways he was real. I remember going to the cemetery for the first time when I was nine. He was there but he wasn't. Part of me wanted to leave and part wanted to dig him up to see him. I wish I could have seen him for real. When I see real men, older men, I ask myself, "Could he be my father for a while? Is this how Dad would walk, talk, smile, laugh, eat?" Sometimes I fantasize that some older man is really my true father. Isn't that strange? I realized that I had never cried for my father, and I probably never would or could. But I hope I do.

Have you cried for your father? Do you need to? Grieving involves being sad not just for a person you knew but also for a person you never had an opportunity to know.

One woman has these memories:

I have so much I wish I could say to my father. Dad was there to a certain extent, but Mom was there more. And sometimes I wanted to be with him, but something always prevented it. When I was sixteen, in fact, the day before he didn't come home from work on time. That was unusual since we could set our clocks by him. Then the police came and told us about the accident. I had nightmares for months because they gave us all the details. I miss him but I'm still angry. I missed out, and I can still hear the sting in his remarks to me and my sisters. How do I get rid of this stuff? He's not here to dump on or just share. Where do I go from here?

GAINING CLOSURE

As I have said, when a woman has lost her father during childhood or adolescence, her grieving will have been incomplete because she didn't have the ability at the time to process the grief.

Although your father isn't around to see or hear you, what I suggest you do is really for yourself and is not dependent upon any other person's response. Write a letter to your father as if he were alive and could read your letter. The only difference is that you might be more explicit in the letter, knowing he isn't going to be reading it. Daughters who have had very positive relationships with their fathers have written letters, sharing how much they loved their father, how much they miss him, and what they wish they would have said to him. Whether your relationship was positive or negative, the result can be the same for you. Once you've written the letter and read it aloud, you don't have to carry these thoughts around anymore in your heart and mind. Write to each of the five categories mentioned below until there's nothing more to say. Put the letter away. Sometime in the future you may want to take it out and read it again.

Unfinished Business

Writing a letter is a way of saying good-bye and eventually gaining closure. In a letter to a father with whom you have unfinished business, *begin by stating the facts*. It's an opportunity to set the record straight from your perspective.

"Dad, you weren't there for me when I needed you. You turned your back on me when I got pregnant and I felt so alone."

"Dad, I never saw you when you weren't angry or didn't have a beer in your hand."

"Dad, you controlled Mother and us so much we couldn't breathe."

"Dad, I needed your affirmation, not your criticism. Why weren't Bs good enough for you?"

One way to face your feelings is to express them. Do this in your letter. *Fully express what you felt or are feeling now* because of certain incidents. Once you begin, you'll find one feeling or thought triggers another.

"Dad, I was so sad much of the time because I wasn't sure if you loved me or not."

"Dad, I felt so guilty and shameful when you caught me kissing Jimmy at ten. It wasn't so much what you said. It was the look you gave me, and then you never talked to me about boys and showed no interest in my boyfriends when I was in high school."

"Dad, I was afraid of you and afraid of how I felt toward you."

"Dad, I'm sorry for blocking you out of my life when you

drank. I didn't know how else to act."

"Dad, I'm just sad that we missed out on so much together."

The third thing to do is to *discuss what might have been*. Talk about what was unfulfilled in your relationship.

"Dad, if we could have talked more I could have learned so much about you, and you could have really known me. I think you would have liked me."

"I wish you would have been nicer to Mom and me."

"I wish you had been more strict with me. You left it all up to Mom, and she couldn't handle me. I needed your firm hand."

"I needed you at my recitals, my birthdays, my games. Were you really always at work, or elsewhere?"

"I have pictures of you, but I don't have your voice. I wish we could have talked."

"I still have scars from the physical abuse. I wish you had been a kind father. That's what I needed, not advice."

Now *share everything you miss about your father*. One way to begin this is to simply write "I miss . . ." ten times or so and then complete each one. You'll be surprised at what comes to mind.

"Dad, I miss hearing you call my name."

"I miss the sound of your laugh."

"I miss the fact that you never met my husband."

"I miss that you never walked me down the aisle."

"I miss the long talks we used to have."

"I miss you now, but I'll see you in heaven."

The last step may feel strange, but it's important: *Bring your father up to date.* You're reintroducing yourself to your father. Tell him what you have done, what you're presently doing, what your hopes and dreams are. Share things about yourself as a child that he wouldn't have known about. If your thoughts or feelings about him have changed over the years, share those as well.

"Dad, you'd be amazed. I don't look like the awkward, stubby girl that you knew. I grew up and I actually look pretty. I have your nose and eyes. I like them."

"I went through four years of college in six, but I made it. One year I made the dean's list. I've been a teacher for five years and love it. I saw how much you loved it, and now I know why."

"Dad, you'd probably be disappointed, but I just got divorced. It just didn't work out."

"Dad, when I was small I didn't understand you. I never heard you laugh much. From what I have learned over the years, now I understand. You're different in my mind now than you used to be."

"You used to think I was perfect, and I didn't want you to think differently. So I didn't tell you about getting caught smoking and ditching school when I was eleven. I can't believe some of the things I did then. I drank a few times in junior high, too."[11]

Some daughters have gone a step further. They write a letter from their father to themselves. It is a healing process for many since it puts them in their father's shoes but also lets them express what they would like to hear from him.

Thankfully, many fathers left a positive influence in their daughters' lives as expressed in our survey.

THANKS FOR ALL YOU DID FOR ME.

"'I love you, Daddy. Thanks for all you did for me. I hope you are in heaven. Thanks for loving me, too.' My father died a month after my husband. The only one left to be my father is God."

"Dad, thank you so much for loving me and showing me the way to Christ. I love you and hope that I can pass this legacy on to my three sons."

"Dad, I'm so thankful God gave me the best dad on earth. It was hard to say good-bye, but I know where you are and that we all will be together again. I will always love you."

Chapter 7

GRIEVING ABSENT FATHERS

Fathers can be absent for many reasons. When a father dies the reason is obvious. When he divorces or abandons the family it's worse than a death. In grief counseling we talk about the various kinds of losses and which are the most difficult to handle. Of all the losses experienced in relationships, *ambiguous* loss is the most devastating kind because it is unclear. There is no certainty or closure about a person's absence or presence.

There are two types of ambiguous loss. One is when a family member is physically absent but is still there psychologically in the hearts and minds of the family members. They have no idea where the person is physically. Traditionally this kind of absence has included runaway or kidnapped children, missing soldiers, or accidents in which the body can't be found. But this can also include absent fathers who have left because of divorce or some other reason. As his child left behind, you wonder, "Where is he?" You never hear from him, and you don't know where he is.

The second type of ambiguous loss is when the person is physically present but psychologically absent. This includes those with addictions, strokes, mental illnesses, comas, or Alzheimer's disease. But this kind of loss could also be expanded to include those who are workaholics and neglect their families—fathers who are there but are absent emotionally. There is no emotional connection. A father is there physically but not really there. In these cases there is often an endless search that goes on—maybe not a physical search, but one within the heart and mind. It feels like a loss to you, but it may not be recognized as such by others.

Sometimes your father comes back into your life for a while, but then leaves again, nowhere to be found. So you alternate between hope and hopelessness. And this kind of loss easily leads to hopelessness. You don't feel completely free to move on. There's always that possibility that Dad might show up . . . but then again, he might not. If your parents are divorced, one parent might not be there physically, but he'll always be there emotionally.

Ambiguous loss also occurs when there are unclear good-byes in daily life. Workaholism is a good example of this. A father can be physically at home, but psychologically he's still at the office. It's difficult for other family members, because even though he's within sight and at home, he's actually absent emotionally and unavailable. Some daughters have said, "I wish he would stay at the office and work. When he's here and working, it sends the message: I'm not important. Work takes first place."[1]

Take a moment to think about your personal sense of loss with regard to your father. The following questions may help.

- As you reflect upon your father, in what ways was he absent from your life?
- If your father left physically, what was the reason for his leaving? Who was most influential in making that decision?
- How old were you at the time, and how did you learn of his leaving?
- Did you think you were the cause of his leaving?
- What are five effects upon your life because of your father's absence?
- With whom did you discuss his going at the time?
- Because Dad left, are there any concerns in your life that others you love may leave?

"It's just too painful. I don't want to believe it and I won't. I have friends who had good dads. Even great dads. There's just too much hurt. I don't want to think about Dad. He hurt me so much. I've been trying to forget him and hoping my heart will heal in time. Isn't that what they say? Time heals all wounds?" Becky is like many women. She would rather not face her father. He's in the past— leave him there, even though there was a lot missing in the relationship. But healing comes through facing what you may call the unacceptable in your life. This was a loss, and all losses need to be faced and grieved over so you can go forward in your life. It's the process that's involved in coming to terms with the hole in your heart and finding peace.

FACING THE PAST

We have to face the past to confront the present. It's not easy. It can be painful. Many are reluctant to "face the unacceptable," as Dr. David Hart describes:

> Many people fear that if they face the unacceptable they will *become* it. The exact reverse is true. If you do not face it, you will become it. It will always be lived out in one way or another. The turning point comes when something in us decides that the unacceptable is really meant for us, and we begin to look for its meaning.
>
> If on the other hand, we employ our usual means not to face what is meant for us—and each of us has his own particular escapes—the terror of the unacceptable not only remains with us, but is also always being lived out as a real disturbance in our lives. We then need constant reassurance that "it is not really so," a precarious and unreal base on which to live.[2]

Dr. David Stoop has suggested several steps in this process. Your *first step* is to identify the symptoms of this loss in your life. These are the places where it hurts. Here are several questions that can help you identify what happened and when.

My relationship with my father in preschool was . . .

_____

_____

_____

My best experience with him at that time was . . .

_____

_____

_____

My worst experience with him at that time was . . .

_____

_____

_____

My relationship with my father in elementary school was . . .

_____

_____

_____

My best experience with him at that time was . . .

_____

_____

_____

My worst experience with him at that time was . . .

_____

_____

_____

My relationship with my father during adolescence was . . .

_____

_____

_____

My best experience with him was . . .

_____

_____

_____

My worst experience with him was . . .

_____

_____

_____

An additional way of identifying symptoms is to look at the men in your life who have been "father figures." Sometimes men are chosen as a means of filling in that hole in your heart left by an absent father. What type of men were they, and what does this say to you?

Finding Your Real Dad

The *second step* in the healing process is to identify what is true about your father and what isn't: What is factual, what has been reinterpreted, and what you don't know about him. Recovery could involve learning some things about your father you would rather not know. As you enter this search-and-discovery phase of your journey, ask God to be your guide as well as an informant. Ask Him to lead you to the truth and the information you need to know.

How do you go about this? First, identify what you would like to know about your father—the questions you need answered. Then go to relatives and friends of your father and simply ask your questions. Ask co-workers also, if any are available. Be aware that you will come up against contradictions as you go through this process.

If your father is available, interview him. Perhaps the use of pictures can help you in this process. Sometimes all it takes is a question. My own father was older than most. He was forty-nine when I was born. I don't remember hearing him say, "I love you." I knew he did because of the way he responded to me. One evening when I was in college I asked him, "Dad, do you love me?"

His answer was, "Of course I love you."

I replied with, "I knew that. I just wanted to hear you say it. Thanks." That one memory is all I need. I'm glad I asked. There are probably questions you have wanted to ask. Do you know what they are?

Exposing Family Secrets

The *third step* in this process can be very enlightening: exposing family secrets and myths. What's the difference between secrets and myths? Dr. David Stoop says, "Myths and secrets are different sides of the same coin. Secrets are the things that happen that we never talk about. Myths are things we talk about that never happened. Both are untruths, and both tend to contradict the understanding and information we have uncovered previously."[3]

Often everyone in the family believes and perpetuates these. Let's take family myths. Can you think of any in your family? If so, who is the one who keeps it going? Sometimes fathers share them about mothers. But most often it's the other way around. Mother becomes the official interpreter of what Father "really meant" or why he did or didn't do something. He's "just working too much"; or "he really wanted to be there"; or "he really loves you more than anyone"; or "he didn't mean it." The problem is, did Dad ever tell you these things, confirming your mom's words? Or do you feel that he would contradict her? Maybe you just accepted the excuses, believing that if your mother told you something, it must be true. And you probably *wanted* to believe it. After all, who would want to believe the opposite?

To discover family secrets, you almost have to be a private investigator. That's why they're called *secrets*. They are what no one talks about. They are usually covered by some deception. Don't expect others in the immediate family to want to talk about them. Sometimes those who are not in the "inner circle" are more likely to talk. What's important is how this family secret has impacted your life. Have you ever asked other family members: "Are there any family secrets I should know about?" It's an important question to ask, especially if it relates to your father. One woman discovered that her father kept two different families at the same time. He was married to two women, had two residences, and all that goes with two families. When this was discovered, it explained the long absences.

Sharing Your Feelings About the Past

The *fourth step* requires a trusted person with whom you can share. It's time to talk about your feelings about yourself, what you've learned, and how you feel about what you've learned. One of the best ways to begin is to *write out* how you feel (longhand rather than on a computer), because the "drainage process" can be very helpful. Sometimes it's best to talk first with a close friend, pastor, or counselor, and then eventually a trusted family member. You may discover you're not alone in your thoughts and feelings.

The *fifth step* is important as well: "Recreate the past."

"Oh, if only it could have been different" is a comment I hear often. It's wistful thinking, but often followed with "Oh well, no sense wasting time on that." But it's not a waste of time. It's helpful to dream about the way you think it should have been because it helps you identify all the things you lost. No one else will do this for you, so you're the one to step out and think about your past. You could do this in a number of ways. You could write the story the way you think it should have been, or you could complete a series of "I wish . . ." statements.

- "I wish my father had . . ."
- "I wish my father hadn't . . ."
- "I wish my father had said . . ."
- "I wish my father hadn't said . . ."
- "I wish my father would say to me today . . ."
- "I wish my father wouldn't say to me today . . ."

I WISH MY

FATHER HAD . . .

Ball of Grief

There can be a host of feelings underlying your losses. The best way to access the feelings you have is to look at your history and identify what you wish were true (which amounts to a loss), then look at the Ball of Grief graphic and identify what you are feeling. If you're angry, write, "I'm angry because . . ." If you're fearful, write, "I'm fearful because . . ." You need to express it in writing—and then give it to God. Say to Him, "God, I'm giving you this. Take it and drain it from my life. I want to move on." Reading other books on loss, grief, anger, or worry can give you other practical steps to take. (See the listing at the conclusion of this chapter.)

You may feel as though you're alone in your grief over your father, and that may be true. There are very few support groups for father loss. It's one of those in which you won't have "a casserole parade" of responses from those who care about your grief. I have seen some women who are able to find others experiencing this loss, and they band together in their own support group. Finding a supportive friend, lay counselor, or professional who understands the grief process can help you move forward. Once you identify your losses, confront each one and don't hesitate to call each one what it is—a *loss*.

Saying Good-bye

The *final step* is to actually grieve. Grief is not an orderly process. It can be disrupted. The following steps have helped others with the grief process.[4]

1. Try to identify what doesn't make sense to you about the losses you experienced with your father. It could be the "why" question, which is both a question and a cry of protest. Even if your father could give you an answer, it probably wouldn't satisfy you. It's like our cry of "Why?" to God. If He ever answered us, we'd probably still argue with Him.

You may wonder, "Did my dad love others?" "I wonder if he had any idea, any guilt over what he didn't do for me?" "When he didn't come to my concert, I wonder if he had any idea how much that hurt me?"

> GRIEF IS NOT AN ORDERLY PROCESS.

One woman shared with me how she overcame her hurt regarding her dad's absence at her concert. She said, "For years I focused on the fact that he wasn't there, and I let that ruin the experience for me. But one day it dawned on me that there were ten other relatives there, as well as my heavenly Father. When I focused on that, my feelings and memories began to change. I had given my father's absence all that power and neglected the others' presence. I had it way out of balance, and I'm able to say now, 'So he wasn't there—but others were.'"

2. Identify your emotions and feelings that you have already thought about or written down. Since this is an ongoing process, do you see any change in their intensity over a period of a few days? Is there an increase or a decrease? Remember, if you're facing some of the new losses for the first time, feelings can be more intense than before.

3. Identify the steps you will take to move ahead and overcome these losses you suffered because of your father. It is helpful to identify what you've done in the past as well.

4. Don't try to handle your losses by yourself. Share this journey with someone else, and remember your journey through grief will never be exactly like that of another person. Yours will be unique.

5. If you know of others who have experienced a similar loss and recovery, talk with them. Their story will have similarities and dissimilarities to yours but could be helpful.

6. Identify the positive characteristics and strengths of your life that have helped you before. Which of these will help you at this time of your life?

7. When you pray, don't hold back any feelings. Share everything you are experiencing.

8. Think about where you want to be in your relationship with your father a year from now. Describe this in as much detail as possible. Put it into a story or letter to yourself, or express it as a prayer to God.

9. Remember that understanding grief intellectually isn't sufficient. It can't replace the emotional experiences of living through this difficult time. You need to be patient and allow your feelings to catch up with your mind. Expect a fluctuation in your feelings and remind yourself that these are normal.

10. One of the most important steps in recovery is being able to *say good-bye*. When you do this, you're acknowledging that you're no longer going to share your life with those hurts, unfulfilled dreams, or expectations. For some, saying good-bye is a one-time occurrence, while others need to do this on several occasions. One of the best ways of doing this is writing a good-bye letter(s) and then reading it aloud as you commit the contents to God. Some find it helpful to wave good-bye to the letter.

When you're able to grieve, you are able to take care of unfinished issues in your life. Not addressing your losses keeps you cemented to the past. Saying good-bye is an important step in this process. Life is a series of hellos, good-byes, and hellos.

How do you feel when you say good-bye? Sadness? A feeling of "I wish it wasn't so," or a sense of relief? The word *good-bye* originally meant *God be with you*, or *Go with God*, and was a recognition that God was a significant part of the passage. It helps to know that as you grieve you will be strengthened when you remember that God is there in your journey with you.

Listen to the words from the writer of *Praying Our Good-byes*:

> We all need to learn to say good-bye, acknowledge the pain that is there for us, so we can eventually move on to another hello. When we learn to say good-bye we truly learn how to say to ourselves and to others: Go. God be with you. I entrust you to God. The God of strength, courage, comfort, hope, love is with you. The God who promises to wipe away all tears will hold you close and will fill your emptiness. Let go and be free to move on. Do not keep yourself from another step in your homeward journey. May the blessing of our God be with you.[5]

When you take the step of saying good-bye, eventually you'll say good-bye to your grief and hello to a new life.

Chapter 8

I'm Not in Denial...or Am I?

———

Wendy came in for counseling about her marriage. But in the first twenty minutes she made three references to her father. I finally asked if she would rather talk about her relationship with her father. She said, "Of course not." She didn't have any problems with her father at all. But her face and body language didn't agree. So I asked, "Tell me a bit about your father. He sounds like quite an interesting individual."

She talked for most of the session about her father, but there were gaps in the story she was telling me. Where there should have been emotion or feeling there was none. I felt as though I was talking with someone in grief, someone who'd had a major loss in her life but couldn't face it. We have a word for that: *denial.* I shared this with her, and there was silence, and then a large sigh. She said, "I guess so. It's been there for a long time."

Many women have become experts at using denial as their means of coping with something that was very unpleasant in the past. Sometimes horrible or hurtful things happened to them as a child, and they didn't want to believe those things ever happened to them. So they switched the channels of the TV in their mind so they wouldn't think about it. If they did think about it, they would see themselves as inferior or having some defect—different than others—and they certainly wouldn't want anyone to know about it. In a way the brain switched off. If it was very bad and traumatic, the brain protected them by shutting off. This is what some refer to as *repressed memories.*

One daughter couldn't handle the fact that her father missed visit after visit with her. So she pretended it wasn't such a big deal. "So he missed a visit . . . it won't happen again." But it did, over and over. But each time it happened it was like the first time. She erased what had happened before, or so she thought. The problem was that it was being filed away in her mind.

Denial is pushing the pain down again and again. It's like pushing a volleyball under the water in a garbage can, letting go, and trying to be quick enough to put the lid on securely in order to keep the ball under the water. But it keeps popping up, coming out of the water, no matter how hard you try to keep it in. Denial is like a heavier version of the volleyball. It sinks for a while, but it slowly floats to the surface, and sometimes you're not even aware it has come to the top. Others may see your pain, but you rely upon the numbness of denial, and while you say, "Everything's all right" with a smile on your face, it really isn't. You say, "It wasn't a big deal"; or "It really wasn't that bad, you're making more of it than it really was"; or "I know others who really had it bad"; or "The Lord took care of that years ago. I hardly even remember it. It doesn't bother me." These statements could be true. I hope they are. But often they're expressions of just the opposite.

KINDS OF DENIAL

Were you aware that there are variations of denial? The following is the range of denial statements, starting with the most serious form.

- *"It never happened."* This is usually said when the event was so painful, so traumatic, or so unbelievable that the mind blanks it out. I've seen it happen in the case of bank robberies, sudden death notifications, rape, incest, and physical abuse. Maybe you heard it wrong. Perhaps you dreamed it or imagined it. You're holding onto hope. The longer you hold on, the more memories fade, the more you can believe that it didn't happen.

- *"It happened, but it had no effect on me."* You admit the event(s) happened, but you were so insulated that whatever happened had no impact on you. But what you experienced did affect you—unless you were Superwoman.

- *"Yes, it did affect me, but it really wasn't that bad."* This belief keeps you from having to deal with the residue of what occurred. "They weren't *that* painful." "Everyone gets rejected at one time or another." "So I was disappointed because he wasn't there. I'm not the only one to experience this." "Dad wasn't gone that much. Sure, I was disappointed, but I remember the one birthday he was there." But not admitting the truth keeps you from moving on with life.

- *"It used to affect me, but not now. I've taken care of it."* This is one of the most common approaches. You think if there are problems in your present life, they have nothing to do with anything connected with the past. It reminds me of a song in the '50s (yes, I was in high school then) called "The Great Pretender." You can't get over what you don't investigate. A doctor can't heal a wound unless he takes a close look at it, cleans it, puts medication on it, binds it up, and continues to check its progress. That's when recovery occurs.

Look these statements over. Do any of them sound familiar?

THE BLAME GAME

Are you familiar with blame? Of course, who isn't? Blame has been with us since the beginning of time. Adam was gifted with this ability. He said, "The woman whom You gave to be with me, she gave me [fruit] of the tree, and I ate" (Genesis 3:12 AMP). He blamed God and Eve, but uttered not a word about himself.

One of the outcomes of moving from denial to accepting the reality of what happened is blame . . . but not necessarily toward your father. Self-blame is common. First, you have the shock of admitting what occurred. Then, like most of us, you search for reasons why it happened so that it makes sense. Unfortunately, when you blame yourself, you hold yourself accountable for what others have done. You may decide that all this happened because:

- You did it! You did something to make it happen.
- In some way you just weren't good enough.
- You didn't do all you could have to keep it from occurring. You could have done more.
- You expected too much or ignored the signs of what might happen, so you're really responsible for your hurt.

YOU COULD HAVE DONE MORE.

Some of the stories I've heard have amazed me. People take responsibility for events in their lives that could not have been their fault in any way, shape, or form. Yet the belief that it was persists. Can you relate to the question *Are you familiar with blame?* Think for a while about events in your life that happened (not only as they relate to your father but to any area of your life) and complete the phrase:

_____ wouldn't have happened if . . .
_____ wouldn't have happened if . . .
_____ wouldn't have happened if . . .
_____ wouldn't have happened if . . .
_____ wouldn't have happened if . . .

What do your answers say about a tendency to accept blame? Would others say you were at fault? In what way were you responsible? Those who have been victims of crimes often blame themselves. Some daughters have said, "If only I had been . . . a better daughter, smarter, more compliant, prettier, born a boy, more open, stronger, shouted more, said no more forcibly. . . ." There are variations of this thought, such as "If only I had not . . ." and these statements express regret. But you weren't to blame. You didn't know back then what you know now, so you can't hold yourself responsible for what you didn't know or couldn't have done. Blame won't help. It doesn't solve problems. When we self-blame, we're punishing ourselves.

Another blaming statement is "I should have known" or "I should have seen it coming."

When we self-blame, we're also saying it wasn't our father's fault or it *couldn't* have been his fault. Why? We don't want to believe that he could have been responsible—that would destroy our image of him. Or it could have been more comfortable to take the blame than to see him as responsible for what happened. We do strange things in order to feel secure. Here's an assignment. Ask those who know you best if you tend to blame yourself. Ask them how often they hear you make statements like:

If only I had . . .

If only I had not . . .

I should have . . .[1]

These are indictments. When you blame yourself, you are acting as a grand jury, issuing an indictment against yourself. Sometimes fathers (for one reason or another) put responsibilities on their daughters that only an adult could accomplish. You tried and tried but never were able to perform as an adult when you were a child. In a sense these messages prevented you from experiencing life as a child. Can you think of any examples of this occurring?

1. _____

2. _____

3. _____

4. _____

Getting Rid of Self-Blame

Sometimes daughters go through life blaming themselves for things a child could never have had any control over. There is a way to overcome these messages or beliefs you created even at this time in your life. The author of *Toxic Parents* has suggested the following exercise. Go into a room where you can be alone, take the following list, and complete aloud each sentence that pertains to you.

"I am not responsible for . . .

. . . the way my dad neglected or ignored me.

. . . the way my dad made me feel unloved or unlovable.

. . . my dad's cruel or thoughtless teasing.

. . . the bad names my dad called me.

. . . my dad's unhappiness.

. . . my dad's problems.

. . . my dad's choice not to do anything about his problems.

. . . my dad's drinking problem.

. . . what my dad did when he was drunk.

. . . the fact that my dad hit me.

. . . the fact that my dad molested me."

Add any other painful, repetitive experiences that you've always felt responsible for. After you've completed this exercise, go back through your list, repeating each item that applies to your childhood, but adapt the statements to read, "My father was responsible for . . ." Be sure to read these aloud.[2]

It is important to remember that you were not responsible for your parents' actions. The only thing you are responsible for is the way you have responded over the years. Can you see how you have allowed the past to influence your present life? You may need to complete the above exercise more than once. But just as an answering machine message can be changed, so can these messages from the past be erased and no longer exert control over your life.

You can stop blaming yourself, if you really want to. One way is to become aware of each and every self-blaming statement you make and then give three separate pieces of evidence to show that your statements are accurate. You need to back up what you say with facts. Every time you make a blaming statement, ask yourself, "Why do I need to blame myself?" Finish this statement at least three times. "I need to blame myself because . . ."

Another way to effect change is to turn every blaming statement into a non-blaming response. If you tend to say, "I should have . . ." change it to "No, I shouldn't have, or couldn't have." If you say, "If only I had . . ." you could say, "No, there's nothing else or anything more I could have done." Counter each negative statement with a positive one several times until it feels comfortable.

START THE HEALING

If you feel you *might* be in denial, where do you go from there? First you admit, "I have been in denial. I don't like to admit it, but it's true. This is what happened" (describe it in detail). "And here are the results" (describe them in detail). You've just invited pain to be a part of your life again, so be careful that you don't slip back into denial in order to numb the pain. But this is how healing begins.

Next, it's important to say the following statements out loud. Then take a piece of paper, write them out in longhand, and then once again say them aloud. It's also important to sit down with a trusted friend and repeat each statement to her. Admitting these things to yourself and to someone else is a great step in the process of healing.[3]

Here are the statements:

"I was hurt."

"What happened to me still hurts."

"That was no way to be treated by anyone."

"It was wrong."

"I've suffered because of what I went through."

"I haven't gotten over it yet."

"It *was* that bad."[4]

If you've been hurt by your father, what is the one thing you would really like to receive from him that you think would make your life better? (Note: It is probably something you will not receive for one reason or another.) It may be a letter of acknowledgment and apology. You may think this is a strange suggestion, but why not write it for him? It doesn't really matter that he's not the one writing it. It may be true that he owes you an apology, but you don't want to wait for one in order to move on. It just might feel good to receive one even if you write it yourself. You know what you would like to hear. Once you have written this, you will have confronted any denial that is there. Here is a sample:

Dear Susan,

I am writing to let you know that I blew it big time. When your mother and I divorced, I wanted to put distance between us. Unfortunately, I did that to you as well. I wasn't upset with you. I love you. And I hurt because I didn't see you much. I let (and I know I'm responsible) your mother's anger get to me, so I didn't come around or call. I realize now that you felt I rejected you and didn't want you. I'm sorry for that. I'm sorry for not being there at important times in your life. I also realize that I hurt myself because I missed out on some wonderful events as well as memories for the future. I wish I could change the past. But I can't. It can be different now if we could begin to build a relationship. I missed out on the past but I don't want to miss out on the future.

> I love you.
> Your father.[5]

Some women who blame themselves feel isolated. They wish they had someone in their corner pleading their case. What happened was wrong. And they feel like they are carrying the burden alone.

You do have someone. You have Jesus, the Son of God. He was abandoned, forsaken, and physically and emotionally abused. He expressed distress, depression, isolation, deep sorrow, and grief at certain times in His life. And He died one of the worst deaths you could imagine. But He's alive today. When you read the Scriptures you discover that He is serving as an advocate for you with God the Father. An advocate is someone who is in your corner. He is someone who speaks for you and maintains your cause. Jesus speaks to the Father about what you have experienced, and that's not all. There's more good news. Because of all that He went through here on earth, combined with His complete knowledge of God, He is the one who can show you the way out of your past. He can show you how to respond, how to turn from denial, and how to face whatever the truth may be, opening up a way for you to move forward in your life.

Chapter 9

CHANGING YOUR RELATIONSHIP WITH YOUR DAD

———

"There is no way I could ever ask my father to change. I wouldn't ask. He wouldn't change. As much as I'd like that, it's not going to happen." This is a cry of frustrated futility coupled with a longing! Beliefs keep us from making a simple request.

"Dad won't change. Our relationship won't change." This belief becomes a self-fulfilling prophecy. It cripples motivation, thwarts desire, and destroys hope.

Consider some of the beliefs that I've heard daughters give for not asking their dad to change:

- *"My father isn't capable of changing."* It's true he might be entrenched in his responses, but could it be you haven't found the right combination to unlock his resistance? The potential for change *is* there.
- *"There's nothing he could do at this point to improve our relationship."* The first question is: Have you identified what you want to be different? Once you know that in specific terms, you'll be able to develop a plan to talk it over.

One daughter just wanted her dad to talk with her for five or ten minutes when she went over to her parents' house. I saw her several weeks after our conversation and asked how the relationship was going. She looked discouraged and said, "Well, I've tried, but not much is working. I've been there more than eight times, and Dad only sat down and talked on three occasions."

I said, "Really? I remember your telling me it wouldn't work, and that's almost a fifty percent improvement. That's quite a step. You must have done something different as well."

She replied, "I guess I was looking at the five times he didn't respond. You're right. Three times was a big step."

I asked, "And the three times he sat down and talked with you—did you thank him for spending the time with you?"

Her response was silence; I had my answer. Be sure you reinforce any change at all on the part of your dad. Thank him. It helps to focus on any positive improvement you see. For you it might not have been much effort to do what your dad did, but for him it was probably a giant step. Look for the exceptions in his typical responses and behaviors. When you choose to look for these, it gives you hope that your father is capable of changing.

- *"If I try something different, it may make matters worse. I don't want to add to the problem."* This usually means, "I have too much pain, and it hurts too much to try." But doing something different doesn't necessarily mean it

IT ISN'T WORTH IT.

will make matters worse. With new information, new understanding, and new approaches, there's a greater possibility that change can happen. If you pay attention to the smallest changes—the slightest difference on your father's part—you could find hope again. If your next attempt to see change doesn't succeed, you may be tempted to think, "I knew it wouldn't work. It isn't worth it." Challenge that thinking. Tell yourself, "All right, it didn't work this time, but at least I tried. Let's see how I can change my response for the next approach."
- *"It's been so many years of this. He's set in cement. The damage is too great."* I've seen some relationships restored that surprised even me. They did look hopeless. Look for the fears that keep you

from responding. Remember, we haven't been called to live in fear. "For God did not give us a spirit of timidity, but a spirit of power, of love and of self-discipline" (2 Timothy 1:7).

It's true! Sometimes the interaction an adult daughter has with her father is consistently less than satisfying. Each time there's a get-together it seems to be a continuation of creating tension and distance rather than improvement and drawing closer.

What about you? What is your interaction like at this time? There are no right or wrong answers, but completing this analysis could help you identify the rough spots, which is the first step in resolving them.

1. Often I can't seem to find the right words to express what I want to say to Dad.
   _____ Yes   _____ No

2. I'm concerned that if I share my real concerns or feelings, I'll end up being rejected by Dad and the door will be shut.
   _____ Yes   _____ No

3. Often I don't say what I really want to because I'm not sure if my opinion is right.
   _____ Yes   _____ No

4. If I speak up, it will only make matters worse rather than better.
   _____ Yes   _____ No

5. I tend to do most of the talking, and Dad doesn't say much.
   _____ Yes   _____ No

6. I don't look forward to face-to-face conversations with Dad.
   _____ Yes   _____ No

7. I don't look forward to phone conversations with Dad.
   _____ Yes   _____ No

8. Once we begin to argue, I keep on going and don't know how to stop.
   _____ Yes   _____ No

9. I tend to blame him and focus on what he did or didn't do in the past.

_____ Yes _____ No

10. I tend to be defensive.

_____ Yes _____ No

11. I have a hard time listening to Dad.

_____ Yes _____ No

12. I respond in like manner to how my father is—anger for anger, insult for insult.

_____ Yes _____ No

13. I rarely bring up significant things to talk about.

_____ Yes _____ No

14. Sometimes I don't share everything, in order to cover the truth.

_____ Yes _____ No

15. I think Dad needs to hear about the problem he's caused.

_____ Yes _____ No

16. When I have a complaint it sounds like anger.

_____ Yes _____ No

17. There are a number of issues I won't bring up with Dad.

_____ Yes _____ No

18. I don't like to argue with Dad since it doesn't accomplish anything.

_____ Yes _____ No[1]

EXPECT RESISTANCE

If you make the choice to ask for change, don't be surprised if you encounter some resistance. Most everyone will resist others' efforts to get them to change. This is especially true for men. People resist change even if it's for their benefit. And there are predictable forms of resistance. Some fathers refuse to listen. They tune out. Their concern is: "If I let her know I've heard the request, I will be expected to change. I'd rather ignore her than have that pressure."

Another response is to agree to change without any intention of doing so. A dad might say, "I'll see. Sounds like a good idea," but it's only a way to placate his daughter. Still another response is a counterattack. Father turns the request around and begins to focus on what his daughter needs to do. He may go into a history lesson of his complaints from years back. One of the worst forms of resistance is to increase or intensify the very thing you're asking him to change. It can be irritating and even humiliating.

Whatever form of resistance you experience, it has one purpose. Your dad hopes you'll give up. Hopes you will abandon the effort. Have you experienced any of these responses in your previous attempts to bring about a change? If so, that may be why you aren't too interested in trying again for change. One of the best ways to reduce your frustration is to give your father, at least in your heart and mind, permission to resist. It's all right. It's normal. And you can handle it. Don't let any form of resistance throw you off. Just be gently persistent.

What do you really want at this time in your life? When you think of building a new relationship with your father, what is it you want to happen? If you want him to somehow make up for what you were lacking in the past, is that really realistic? Is it even possible? And if he did that, how would that really change your life or fulfill you? The past cannot be changed. But you *can* do something about the present and the future. You can create present and future change. One of the ways to determine what you want to happen is by completing three sentences, stating the way things are right now.

I am . . .

_____

_____

You are . . .

_____

_____

We are . . .

_____

_____

Now ask yourself how you would like the relationship between you and your father to be if everything were perfect.

If our relationship were perfect:

I would . . .

_____

_____

You would . . .

_____

_____

We would . . .

_____

_____

How does this compare with how your relationship looks at this time? Is it realistic, or are there huge gaps between the two? To bring a balance to your responses, complete these three sentences.

Realistically:

I could . . .

_____

_____

You could . . .

_____

_____

We could . . .

_____

_____

Now think of what you could do to make this a *reality*. Reconciliation won't just happen magically. There are several factors to consider.

How will you approach your father if he is someone you have had difficulty with over the years (and perhaps you have punished in your mind)?

What exactly will be your opening remarks, and then what would you like to say to your father and what would you like your father to say to you?

How are you feeling about approaching your father? Are you afraid? If so, what do you think causes this fear? Perhaps there are conflicting emotions and attitudes. You must identify these, because they could cripple your efforts.[2]

Giving Up the Dream

A woman who is struggling with a very difficult father often bristles or becomes angry or sits back in a defensive posture when I suggest the need to accept that individual as he is. Her perception of acceptance may involve liking or approving of what the other person does. But that's not it at all.

Acceptance can simply mean giving up the dream of your father changing or becoming who you would like him to be. After you have creatively and patiently taken the steps we have suggested, you may find that your father is determined not to change. Even when people want to change, they may feel incapable of doing so. Instead of fighting it, you can choose to accept your father's resistance or incapacity to change.

I recently made this suggestion to a woman who was telling me about her dad's latest phone call. Judy had initially come in for counseling because of her struggle to cope with a critical and non-affirming father. Every phone conversation ended with his negative remarks aimed at her. Judy would be upset for days, have difficulty sleeping, and take out her anger on those around her.

In an attempt to resolve this impasse, I began asking some questions: "Judy, how often does your father call you each year?"

"Maybe twenty to twenty-five times."

"How many of the calls are the way you would like them to be? How often is your dad positive, not critical, perhaps even affirming?"

Judy hesitated a minute and said, "You may find this hard to believe, but I would say maybe one phone call a year. That's all, just one."

"So overall, how would you describe your father over the past few years, negative or positive?"

"Negative. I've shared that with you ever since I have been coming here. He is so critical."

"But you *expect* him to be positive when he calls. Is it realistic for you to expect that with the past history you've described for me?"

"No, I guess not."

"So why be surprised when he's negative? He's usually this way, and you've survived each phone call, even though it's been upsetting."

Judy actually finished what I was going to say: "So, I ought to just figure this is Dad being Dad. Why should I expect anything different at this point unless there's some dramatic change in his life? He's who he is."

I also suggested that, in her heart and mind, Judy should try to give her father permission to be who he is—to be negative. If she could learn to respond to his criticism in new ways, she would be better able to cope with the painful interaction. Accepting her dad as he is and giving him permission to be a certain way could significantly free her to move ahead in whatever relationship they might have.

Then I asked Judy one more question: "When your father is positive and affirming that one time during the year, do you compliment him? Do you say something like, 'Dad, thanks for being so positive and affirming today. It meant so much to me'?"

Judy sat quietly and then said, "No, I guess I never have."

All I said was, "It's worth doing. You may be surprised at the results."

This is the beginning of the change process.

REQUESTING A CHANGE

There are several steps to take when requesting a change. First of all, consider making it in writing. Men respond so much better to written instructions and/or concerns. They understand the written word better since they tend to be visual learners. And this gives them time to mull over the request for a while. It keeps them from arguing with you and may prevent a quick, negative response to the request.

Try to make just one request each time. If you bring up several, it's an overload and overwhelms him.

Were you aware that there are positive intentional statements that you could make in ten seconds or less? And it doesn't have to be an abundance of words either. A principle you could follow is found in Proverbs 25:11 (AMP), "A word fitly spoken and in due season is like apples of gold in a setting of silver."

In today's vernacular we could say, "The right word at the right time, how good it is." And it's not only important *what* you say, but *how* you say it.

Be bottom-line and specific in what you're requesting. Words that are vague or general can be confusing. And point to the desired behavior rather than focusing on what someone hasn't done. Requests like the following don't work well:

- "You never spend time with me."
- "You don't seem to listen to me."
- "You don't show an interest in my job."
- "Why is it you never want to talk about the divorce with me?"

Your father will probably defend himself with an isolated example of when he gave the desired response. And he feels attacked as well. Remember to point toward the desired behavior. Your father won't feel attacked, and the request carries with it the unspoken statement "I believe you can do it!" Here are some examples:

- "Dad, I really appreciate it when you spend time with me. When that happens I feel special."
- "Dad, I appreciate it when you listen to me when I'm sharing something and let me know you've heard me. I feel closer to you when that happens."
- "Dad, it really helps me when you ask how I'm doing in my job. It gives us more to talk about, and I feel more like an adult."
- "Dad, I have a number of questions about the divorce. I know it might be painful to talk about it, but when you're ready, I'd like to listen. This would help me understand myself better."

Notice that these statements point to the behavior you want as well as let him know how you feel, which can help him understand.

Give Him Some Time

Keep in mind that most men like to have some time to mull over their answer instead of being put on the spot and asked for an immediate response. If your father's personality is that of an introvert, don't expect him to respond immediately to your questions. Introverts need to think before they speak, and they need silence around them to help them process their answers. They often take seven to ten seconds to answer a question, so if you don't have an immediate response, don't assume he hasn't heard you or he's ignored you. Don't repeat your question. Give him time.

What if your father begins to object and tries to argue? This is where you stand your ground. The way in which you do this is important. You can be calm, definite, and persistent, even if your father is loud or irate. It helps to learn to use the "broken record" technique. I realize that today with cassettes and CDs, there are some who have never seen a vinyl record. Records came in three speeds—78, 45, and 33⅓ RPM. As the vinyl disk went around on the turntable, the needle would sometimes get stuck in a groove or crack and some phrase would be repeated again and again. This is where the statement "you sound like a broken record" came from.

When you use this approach, repeating what you have to say (whether it's an answer or a request) again and again, regardless of what Dad says, eventually he will begin to yield. Just come back and repeat your request with a proper tone of voice. If you are responding to an unreasonable request on his part, repeat, "No, I'm unable to do that," and eventually it works.

When you're asked for other reasons (and you will be), just repeat the same statements. You don't have to give your reasons. If you do, you will be handing Dad more power. This broken record technique may be different for you, but it works, and it could surprise your father.[3]

BE DIFFERENT. DO THE UNEXPECTED.

Be Creative

Part of building a better relationship with your father is establishing better boundaries. It may take time and several attempts to build a better relationship. In many cases you may not need to bring up past issues to build a better present. You can't change past issues, and you can't extract payment. (Some issues do need addressing, however.) If you dread talking or getting together, but it's a necessity, don't do so with negative expectations; you could make them come true. Be different. Do the unexpected. Be friendly. Don't get hooked into old communication patterns. Ignore it when you're baited to repeat past issues or discussions. All families have unspoken rules of behavior and communication. Change them. Violate the rules in a healthy way. Give a different greeting. Ask different questions. Talk to others in a different way. If you're an expander (loads of detail), condense. If you're a condenser (brief, one word responses), expand and give loads of detail. Don't ask standard questions or those that elicit a simple yes or no response. If you usually sit, stand. If you usually stand or walk around, sit. Sit in different chairs. Take a different chair at dinner. Arrange the table differently. Will it work? It may create a different atmosphere, or it may not. It's worth the effort.

Show your father you're different. If you do something different, it can throw him, and you won't have to play the old family games.

The reason any game continues is that you have players. So don't play. Break the pattern. When you see your dad, do you walk in the age you are now—or are you a six-, twelve-, or sixteen-year-old in his presence?

Genevieve shared her experience. "Usually when I drop over to see my parents, Mom comes to the door and greets me; we talk a bit and then she says, 'Go in the family room and say hello to your dad. He's watching TV, as usual.' That's what I've done for years. He grunts a greeting, says a couple of words; I try to commit, and it's a waste. So I said, 'No Mom, if he wants to talk with me he can do it out here away from the TV.' So I went into the kitchen. He knew I was there. In fifteen minutes he came in and said, 'Hey, how come you didn't come in and say hello?' I just said, 'Hi, Dad. It's good to see you. Sit down and tell me which novel you're reading now.' And it worked. He sat. We talked. It was the best conversation we've had in years."

One day I talked with another woman about her father. She said, "I'd like to talk to my father about my childhood and all the stuff I've dealt with."

"What's your purpose in talking with him?" I asked.

"Well, I'd like him to really understand how he impacted my life. He's clueless. He needs to know what he did and how I ended up feeling."

"Does *he* need to know, or do *you* need for him to know?"

"Hmmm . . . I guess it's the latter. But he should understand that I felt like I was growing up without a father . . . and that shouldn't have happened."

"So, what do you want from him now, since you can't change or rewrite the past?"

"I guess I want him to admit what I said . . . that he wasn't there for me and that influenced my life . . . and not in the best ways."

"What if he won't admit that? What if he doesn't see it that way, and what if he says, 'I did the best I knew how'? What then? Where does that leave you?"

"I just hope he will. I'm not sure . . ."

"If he doesn't admit it, does that mean you will allow his refusal to continue to control you—to influence you? Is your ability to move on in life dependent on your father's responding the way you want him to?"

Silence.

Establish Your Purpose

Many daughters find themselves at this point. They want to reconnect with their father, but is their purpose just to make contact, to win some admission, or is it to actually gain reconciliation with him? If it's reconciliation you're after, you will need to give your father time to process what you are sharing. Remember what we said a few paragraphs back: Men need time to mull over information, especially if it involves their feelings. Perhaps you've been distanced from your father for some time either physically or emotionally. Or could it be you would just like to improve your relationship?

If your purpose is reconciliation, then proceed with two intentions: one, to improve the relationship, and the other, to share your perspective. Make sure it's not to punish him or to walk out of his life forever. Before you meet, write out what you would like to say and then read it aloud.

How has your father responded to you in the past? With silence, criticism, blame, anger, walking out? Why should you expect anything different now? You're the one who wants it different, and you probably have better skills to make it happen as well. You want the change. Be willing to hear his side. If you have a quiet father, there's a lot you don't know. A number of adult daughters throughout our country were amazed by what they heard from their World War II veteran fathers after they saw the movie *Saving Private Ryan*. The experience brought back a flood of memories to many men who had been traumatized in the war and had never received any help. They lived with horrible visual and auditory memories locked inside of them for years. One daughter said:

> I do not want to paint too grim a picture of life with an
> alcoholic father. There was a moment of truth I have had

about his memory since his death. This moment has helped the emptiness in my heart about him.

He was a Navy lieutenant in World War II. When I saw the movie *Saving Private Ryan*, it affected me for days. Then I remembered my mother's words, "Your dad was never the same when he came home from the war. It changed him, and he could never talk about it." That movie sparked in me a compassion and understanding of why he turned to alcohol and lived a wasted life. It broke the hardness on my soul about his memory.

Both you and your father have a point of view that is valid. Meet with your father with the attitude "What can I learn about Dad and myself from our get-together?"

When you meet with your father, state your purpose. Point toward what you want. Blame only activates defensiveness in a man.

Here are some sample statements:

- "Dad, I would like our relationship to be better. I want to work toward that and wondered if you would help me in the process."
- "Dad, I would like to talk with you about us. There are some areas that trouble me, and I want to make it better."
- "Dad, I have some questions I've never asked before. It would help me to understand you and help us if I could ask them."

Now you've stated your purpose. The next step may be a bit more difficult for you. It's taking responsibility for your own part in making the relationship what it was.

- "Dad, I think I expected too much from you in the past. I'm letting go of these expectations, and we can see where we go from there."
- "Dad, I know it must have been painful for you the year I didn't respond to your messages. I don't want that to happen again."
- "Dad, I said some hard things to you when I was in college. I didn't understand what was going on in your life. I'm sorry for what I said."

The next step is future oriented. Make a statement about what you would like your relationship to be in the future. This is not about placing blame or rehashing the past. It's a positive description of the changes you would like to see occur.

- "Dad, I'd like us to be able to sit down and talk about significant topics whenever I come over."
- "Dad, there's a lot I don't know about you when you were growing up and what happened in Vietnam. I'd have a more complete picture of who you are if you could share that with me. And I'll really listen."
- "Dad, I want us to move on and have a fresh start. We both missed connecting with each other, and I think we can now."
- "Dad, I'm so glad the drinking and drug years are over for both of us. We're both different now, and it's going to be better. I really like it when you call to see how I'm doing, and I will do the same with you."[4]

Change is possible. This is how some daughters changed themselves and/or their relationship with their fathers:

The biggest thing that was lacking was the inability to talk to Dad about anything important. I've overcome this by making sure that my kids can talk to me about anything. I don't want them to feel that they can only discuss the superficial stuff with their parents. Another thing that was lacking with my father was that while I always knew I was loved, neither he nor Mom ever told me they loved me (or any of the other kids). I'm trying now to tell my kids—right out loud—that I love them. It's not easy saying it out loud when you grow up never hearing it.

I've accepted that I can't go back to change the past, and that it has helped to make me who I am today—for better or for worse. I choose not to believe the lies my father taught me both with his actions and his words. I make this choice as often as I have to for me to believe the truth.

Throughout my walk, I have done several things in an attempt to overcome this. I have prayed and studied Scripture. I have tried to understand my father's situation. For example, I have considered: What was his home life like? What were his unmet needs? What kinds of stresses and burdens did he carry in trying to raise a large family on an unpredictable income? How much praise and encouragement has he received throughout his life? Why were his fears and insecurities so strong? I have sought the influence and wisdom of solid Christians (male and female). Finally, I have also gone through some counseling. Prior to counseling, I know that I spent years trying to convince myself that my experiences did not justify my feelings of loss, sadness, anger, or aloneness because I knew that other people had experienced much more traumatizing situations. I tried to convince myself that the intensity and depth of my feelings were unjustified because I hadn't experienced physical abuse or sexual abuse and that my trials really were minor in comparison to many others'.

I also told myself that God had provided multiple individuals to be paternal figures for me, and thus, I really had no reason for feeling alone or sad. "My experiences really weren't a big deal," I had told myself. The counseling has allowed me to admit that, for me, my situation *was* a "big deal" and that it was painful and difficult. Admitting this allowed me to purge a great deal of sadness that I didn't even realize existed and to have more forgiveness in my heart. The counseling and the influence of the male Christian role models whom the Lord has put in my life have allowed me to see more realistically who Christ has made me to be and into whom He continues to make me. This has been extremely freeing and exciting. I know that the Lord has grown me and healed me a great deal. Yet I also know that this sense of coasting still exists at a certain level. I continue to try to make Christ my anchor.

Our relationship was lacking at one time, but one day I told myself to confront my dad with my issues. We had so many unresolved issues, some very painful. We cried as I asked my dad many questions. I needed answers too, but it turned out to be very rewarding: We finally were Father and Daughter.

As I grew older I reached out to my dad with words and acts of love. In the end, when he was dying, I was the one he called to share his feelings with.

Letting Go

To let go doesn't mean to stop caring
    it means I can't do it for someone else.
to let go is not to cut myself off
    it's the realization that I can't control others.
to let go is to admit powerlessness
    which means the outcome is not in my hands.
to let go is not to try to change or blame another,
    I can only change myself.
to let go is not to care for
    but to care about.
to let go is not to judge
    but to allow him to be human.
to let go is not to deny
    but to accept.
to let go is not to criticize and regulate anyone,
    but to try to become what dream I can be.
to let go is not to regret the past,
    but to grow and live for the future.
to let go is to fear less and love more!
    —Author unknown

Chapter 10

GIVE GOD YOUR MIND

———

I would like to change the past. I wish there was a button on me like my VCR that would erase all that was recorded before. I've tried one way and another to change it. I used to believe I wasn't good enough, so I became "good" enough, but that didn't change it. Then I began to punish myself for whatever I might have done back then, but all that happened was misery. It didn't fill any void. Whatever was wrong in the past I was trying to make right and it didn't work. I went down one road and then another but they led nowhere. So tell me: How do I fix this hole in my heart about my father?

"Forget it. Just forget it and get over it." "You've got to forget what happened and move on with your life." These are admonitions from others that we buy into, but we need to say no to them. Forgetting is not the key to forgiveness. Remembering is. Let's illustrate this with a conversation a good friend of mine, and therapist, Dave Stoop had with one of his counselees:

Myra burst into tears. I have seldom heard anyone sob so deeply. I was at a loss to understand this sudden outburst; I had no idea what had caused it. So I sat quietly and waited.

"I can't, that's all," she said. "I just can't."

"You can't what?" I asked gently.

Silence. By now in our discussions I had learned that Myra's father had physically and sexually abused her from the time she was eleven years old until she ran away from home at seventeen. Later Myra had married a fine man named Greg, a widower with one son; they now had a daughter of their own. Their marriage was good. They appeared to be a happy family.

Myra had come to me for counseling because she wanted to get free of the bitterness and resentment she felt toward her father. We had met together a few times, and she seemed to be coming to grips with her misery-filled childhood. But today before we had even gotten started, the tears had begun to flow.

"Myra, *what* can't you do?" I asked again.

She slowly lifted her head and looked at me through tear-filled eyes. "I can't forget what he did to me," she sobbed. "I've tried. I've really *tried*. But I just can't!" She buried her head in her hands and wept quietly.

I waited for a moment, then said simply, "But Myra, you don't have to forget."

She looked up at me again, a bewildered look on her face. "Say that again," she said.

"You don't have to forget what your father did to you," I repeated.

"But . . . then how can I . . . I mean . . ." Myra stammered.

"Myra," I asked, "who told you that you had to forget what happened?"

She pulled back in her chair, really confused now. "Why—why the Bible says so. Doesn't it?"

"I've never read that in the Bible anyplace," I said.

"But . . . it must. I mean . . . the people at church . . . everyone says . . ."

"I know," I said. "Everyone says, 'Forgive and forget.' I don't know where that old saying comes from, Myra. But it definitely doesn't come from the Bible. And to tell you the truth, it's not very good advice. I don't *want* you to forget what happened, Myra. If anything, I want you to *remember*."

Myra just sat there. She obviously did not know what to make of what I was telling her.

"Listen," I said. "Have you ever burned your fingers?" She nodded silently. "And it hurt, didn't it?" She nodded again. "Well, Myra, what would happen if you ever forgot how it hurt, or how you did it?"

"I guess I'd be liable to burn my fingers again," she said. I could see the light of understanding beginning to dawn in her eyes.

"That's exactly right!" I said. "That's one of the things our memory does for us. It helps us learn from the past so that we don't have to repeat painful mistakes."

"Now, Myra," I said, "we've talked a lot about forgiving your father. I've told you how important forgiveness is. But listen to me; I do want you to *forgive* your father, but I do not want you to *forget* what he did. Forgiveness has nothing to do with forgetting. Do you understand? *Forgiveness has nothing to do with forgetting.*"[1]

REMEMBER . . . THEN FORGIVE

This is where forgiveness begins—with remembering. You can never change what has happened to you in the past, but you *can* change how you respond to it.

FORGIVENESS BEGINS WITH REMEMBERING.

When you accepted Christ, you became a new creation in Jesus Christ. You are now identified with Him. Paul, in 2 Corinthians 5:17, says: "Therefore, if anyone is in Christ, he is a new creation; the old has gone, the new has come!" Then in Romans 6:6 (NASB): "Our old self was crucified with Him . . . that we should no longer be slaves."

By believing in Jesus Christ, we've died with Him and have been raised a new creation in Him. *All* things are new. In what way are you new today? How can your mind—your thought life—and the influence of your past experiences with Dad become new to your life now? First Corinthians 2:16 tells us, "We have the mind of Christ." In 1 Corinthians 1:30 we read, "It is because of him that you are in Christ Jesus, who has become for us wisdom from God— that is, our righteousness, holiness and redemption." You and I have the *wisdom* of God. Put this thought together with the fact that we have the mind of Christ: *Not only do I have the mind of Christ, but I also have God's wisdom to apply in using the mind of Christ in my life.* That will make a difference.

The Ghosts of Our Past

This is very important. Why? Because one of the struggles in which we all engage is with the ghosts of our past. Scripture speaks of this as the "old self" (Romans 6:6 NASB). The mind of our old self has been programmed with our early experiences. But even before this we came into life with a mind that was affected by the fall of man. Thus we begin life with a mind that has a propensity toward negative thinking, worry, fear, guilt, and remembering experiences that would be better off relinquished. Even when we become believers, the residue—the ghost—of old thinking is still with us. It tends to bring its influence into play with our will, our emotions, our thoughts, and our behavior.

Do you live in the present, or do you spend more of your time as a visitor in the past? Some women do, especially if there was a time when there were happy memories of Dad. It's easy to escape to the past when life gets tough in the present. When something you had for a while was wonderful and then it disappeared, it's easy to create a radar lock on those happy times. I've talked to some who speak of their past relationship in such glowing terms, you wonder if it was real. One author said, "Some may tell themselves that the world of the past was the best world ever possible, and that such a pleasant life will never happen again except in the re-creation of their memories."[2]

Oswald Chambers made a remark about death: "The Bible never

allows us to waste time over the departed. It does not mean that the fact of human grief is ignored, but the worship of reminiscence is never allowed."[3]

For some it's not just reflecting on a memory; the memory begins to dominate the present and hinders one from moving ahead. When the past prevents progress, it could be a case of "the worship of reminiscence." What new memories have you created for yourself during the past year? What are the memories you want to create during the coming year? These are questions that can help you move forward and avoid being hopelessly stuck in the past.

Our hurts from the past with our father could be like abscesses—raw, hemorrhaging wounds that become covered with scabs. But from time to time the scabs peel off. Unfortunately, what is uncovered is not the complete growth of restored life, but the same bleeding sore.

Many women travel through life with unhealed emotional wounds. They carry them in their memories. The capacity for being affected by our past actually increases with age, for the older we get, the more we have to remember. Our life in one degree or another is a reflection of our memories. The feelings we have at the present time—such as joy, sorrow, anger, grief, and contentment—are more dependent upon the way we remember an event than the event itself. The greater the length of time between the event and the present, the greater the potential for distortion. Who we are today is a product of how we remember past events. I heard Dr. Lloyd Ogilvie aptly describe the condition in a Sunday morning message:

> We mortgage the future based upon what happened in the past. We have positive memories of the past which we can't imagine could ever be repeated and we have negative memories which we know will be repeated.
>
> Often we become the image of what we remember instead of what we envision for the future.

Our emotions and their intensity are related to memory. Henri Nouwen said, "Remorse is a biting memory, guilt is an accusing memory, gratitude is a joyful memory and all such memories are deeply influenced by the way we have integrated past events into our way of being in the world. In fact, we perceive our world with our memories."[4]

Did you ever think of the possibility that much of the suffering of a person's life comes from her memories? They can produce strong feelings, such as loneliness, insecurity, fear, anxiety, and suspicion. The reason they hurt is because they tend to be mostly buried, emerging only when they choose. The more painful these memories are, the more hidden and repressed they become. They hide, as it were, in a corner of the deepest cavern of our minds. And because they're hidden, they escape healing.

Healing for Painful Memories

What do you do with a painful memory? You may try to forget it, or you may act as though it did not occur. Trying to forget the pains of the past gives these memories power and control over your life, and you proceed through life dragging a weight. You become a walking emotional cripple. You attempt to edit your own personal history and try to selectively remember, but there is a twofold cost: You continue to limp through life, and you miss out on opportunities to grow and mature.

It doesn't have to be this way. A painful memory can become a healed gift instead of a searing reminder. How does healing occur? By facing your memories, remembering them, and letting them out of their closet. Henri Nouwen said, "What is forgotten is unavailable and what is unavailable cannot be healed."[5]

The healing of an intensely painful memory is difficult because of defenses we've built around it to keep us from directly confronting that ghost from the past. In our minds we raise a drawbridge to keep the enemy out, but we end up keeping others away from us as well. This limits us from enjoying deep intimacy, trust, and love. Raising the drawbridge doesn't make our castle more secure; instead, it turns our sanctuary into a dungeon. To heal our hurts of the past with Dad, we need to lower the drawbridge by giving up our defense mechanisms and confronting the painful memories.

We can let down the drawbridge because of the presence of Christ in our lives. He gives us two possibilities for growth and happiness: First, He changes the old patterns by eliminating the effects of harmful memories. Second, He helps us use our minds, emotions, and wills to behave in a new, more positive way both now and in the future.

Our task then, through Christ, is to remove the rough edges and fissures that drain our energy and keep us from moving forward. Christ is the Master Sculptor who renews us after His image (see Colossians 3:10).

Memory Banks

In order to let God work on us, we need to see what went into the making of who we are now. Our view of who we are began in infancy. Smiles or frowns, slaps or pats, reaffirming or sarcastic comments from our father and others were all filed in our emotional memory banks. These memory banks become our warehouses of beliefs, feelings, and impressions upon which we draw throughout our lifetime. Some items in our memory banks are potentially harmful, and they will stay with us unless we take definite steps to replace them with others. Some people's memory banks send them into the world with many pluses, and life is good to them. Others' memory banks send them out with deficits, and life is a constant struggle for them.

The image that is formed by the words and actions of others throughout our childhood reflects how we see ourselves—as worthy or unworthy of respect and love, competent or useless, likable or distasteful, successful or a failure. We tend to respond according to what is stored in our memory banks. One mother noticed that when visitors came to their home she became short and impatient with her children. As she talked about this with me she discovered that her problem was not so much impatience with her children as it was fear of rejection by the visitors if her children did not behave and measure up to standards she set for them. Where did this fear come from? From her own past experiences of rejection.

Janet shared with me that she usually contradicted her husband,

Bill, when he complimented her. She could not seem to accept his positive statements. This was very frustrating to Bill. As she was contradicting him one day, she began to remember comments her parents had made to her. They told her not to believe positive statements that others said about her, because those people just wanted to use her in some way. They also told her the statements were not true anyway, because she didn't have anything to offer. These painful memories blocked her ability to accept her husband's love and care.

Whenever Jan talked to her husband, she would get loud and angry if he happened to turn his head or look away for any reason. She could not understand why she became irate at his seeming inattention. During a prayer session one day she remembered that her father rarely listened to her and usually left the room when she was talking. Her fear of not being listened to by her husband came from this experience with her father. Through prayer and talking this through with her husband, she was able to put those experiences and memories in perspective.

June was in her late twenties. Her father lived a thousand miles away, and she hadn't seen him in several years. Not only that, he hadn't called and neither had she. On one hand June seemed to be quite logical about her relationship or lack of one with her father. She said, "I have several choices: Wait for him to call; I call him; I forget him and stuff my feelings; or I get over him and get a life. But to do that I'd need to forgive him, and I don't think he deserves it, or . . . I wish I could be healed of this mess like Jesus used to heal people."

I said, "Could you explain?"

"Well, for years I imagined that I was there. You know, during the New Testament times when Jesus was there and I could see Him and hear Him. One day, just like the little girl He touched and she rose from the dead, Jesus touched me and I rose—not from the dead, but my heart was whole—the pain from my father was gone, it was lifted. Jesus' love and His touch give life. He touched so many women and healed them of something. And every woman was a daughter. He raised up Peter's mother-in-law who was sick, a woman with an issue of blood, a twelve-year-old girl was given her life back, and it goes on and on. My favorite that I read over again and again is in Luke 8; Jesus took hold of her hand and called, saying, 'Little girl, arise.' Then her spirit returned and she arose immediately. Her father interceded for her. I don't have a father who would do that for me. I wish I did."

I replied, "But, you do. You have someone who wants to touch that wound in your heart and close it so the pain and heartache is no more. It's Jesus himself. Ask Him to do just that. Believe that He is doing it. Close your eyes and just use your gift of imagination, see Him touching your heart. See the hole closing. Ask Him to continue to touch your heart. Give Him all the residue you've gathered over the years. You don't need it."

TRUE HEALING IS IN JESUS

This is where true healing takes place—in the presence of Jesus. The daughter in Luke had died physically and was raised. Many women died emotionally as children, and they need to be raised from their deathbeds as well. It can happen! The words in Luke, "Little girl, arise" are for you as well. Jesus can heal and resurrect wounded daughters who became women, but died emotionally.[6] Your emotions and feelings that have been so bothersome, your beliefs and attitudes that have been crippled, can be changed.

We may already be aware of a particular memory and its effect on us. But sometimes it may take some digging to search it out. Psychologists and counselors are often instrumental in helping people uncover painful memories. But as a Christian you can call on another source. You can call upon the Holy Spirit to bring to mind the disturbing memories that need to be healed. You do this through a quiet time of praying, asking the Holy Spirit to reveal the situation that created the memory in the first place. He may show you the first incident that occurred, or He may show you the first time you responded to the original event.

As you make your request in prayer, you then need to sit quietly, allowing free-floating thoughts to come to your awareness. You shouldn't *try* to make thoughts emerge but rather relax and allow the Holy Spirit to work. If you are attempting to discover situations from the past that correspond to present responses, you could take one person at a time from your childhood and ask, "Did this ever occur with my father?"

The Holy Spirit may reveal a pattern in your behavior with many people. And as you trace this pattern back, you can discover the origins. You are not looking for the source in order to blame yourself or anyone else. You are looking at your own memories to allow the artistry of the Holy Spirit to correct the blemishes.

When a memory is discovered, your first request to the Lord is to give you the grace to thank Him for that memory. It's an emancipation! You're experiencing the first step toward freedom. You now have the unique opportunity to be free from the control of the past.

But the experience can also be a bit frightening. Fortunately, we do not go through it alone, for God is with us. We can consider the hurt of the past as tragic and permanently crippling emotionally. In other words, we can choose to be a slave to it or we can choose to be freed from it. Paul says, "So then, brethren, we are under obligation, not to the flesh, to live according to the flesh" (Romans 8:12 NASB), and "It was for freedom that Christ set us free; therefore keep standing firm and do not be subject again to a yoke of slavery" (Galatians 5:1 NASB).

There is freedom in the Spirit, and it comes from Jesus Christ, who went to the cross for our sins, our emotions, and our memories as well. "What then? Shall we sin because we are not under law but under grace? May it never be!" (Romans 6:15 NASB). Being alive to Christ, fully alive, means being dead to our memories of pain. The healing of memories may be immediate, but often it is progressive. Inner healings can take months or even years. The greater the amount of buried material, the slower the process. This is healthy. We are limited in what we can confront at one time. It could be that experiencing all the hurt of the experience at once would be intolerable. We can only handle one draining sore at a time, and when that is healing, we can move to the next.

First Steps

Another reason for facing one memory at a time is that you need to develop new ways of responding and behaving. Like a child, your first steps may be halting and tentative. Attempting too much at once could discourage you. As you establish new thoughts and ways of behaving, you are encouraged to confront additional areas. When you become fully aware of a painful memory, the intensity of the hurt will diminish a little each day as you think about it. Soon it is no more than an historical remembrance. The more you are willing to express thankfulness and forgiveness, the sooner the hurt will leave.

Pray that God will show you the impact the look of a father has had on your life. Monique Robinson, author of *Longing for Daddy*, said it took five years of God working in her life for healing to occur. In her chapter "A Message From a Fatherless Daughter" she said:

> My life was transformed. My mind reshaped. I gained joy and peace as I learned to lean on my Daddy—God. I viewed Him as my Father and treated myself as His beautiful daughter. Recognize God as your real Father. Get on your tiptoes, stretch, and reach for *the* Father. . . . Discover His love and affection. He can and wants to be present in your life.
>
> Our Father in heaven has everything we need. He can fill every need that He designed our fathers to fill. David, in Psalm 68:3, reminds us that God is a father to the fatherless.
>
> Feed on the promises of God, for He cannot lie, and His Word will not return void. Cling to His promise in Psalm 27:10, for our heavenly Father will take care of you.
>
> God wants to tuck you in bed at night, be the shoulder you cry on, wipe away your tears, hold and care for you, walk hand in hand with you. Invite Him to be there for you as a Father. God won't impose; God only comes when invited.[7]

In what way would you like your life to be transformed?

_____

_____

In what way would you like your mind to be reshaped?

_____

_____

What will it take for you to see God as your Father?

_____

_____

Honoring Your Parents

There is one last step that may be a surprise. If we're going to follow Scripture, there is one passage that could be difficult for wounded daughters. But we must not resist it. Ephesians 6:2–3 reads, "Honor your father and mother"—which is the first commandment with a promise—"that it may go well with you and that you may enjoy long life on the earth." Many daughters not only say "No" or "That can't apply to me," but get angry at the very thought of it. I don't know how you respond to this, but let's just look at the teaching. Remember that honoring is like forgiveness. It's a process of learning to do it. And honor is not conditional, as in: "If your father did or didn't . . . then you honor him." It says honor no matter what—which means to revere, to show respect, to show a continuous regard for. But this will take time, and you won't be able to do it yourself. Being able to obey this Scripture will happen because of the Holy Spirit's working in your life.

HONOR IS NOT CONDITIONAL.

Honoring doesn't mean reunion or reconciliation. There are many possibilities. It may mean giving up anger or resentment and making peace with him _in your mind_. We rail on people more in our mind than we do face-to-face. It could mean reaching out to your father first, accepting the fact that he may never acknowledge what he did or didn't do, or it may mean accepting his apology without saying all those things you've wanted to say for years. It could be one or all of these. When we rehearse what we want to say again and again in our mind, most often the thoughts are negative, angry, or both. Rehearsing them doesn't affect your father, but it does affect you. It doesn't tear him down, but it tears down your spirit and attitude, and affects your body and physical health.

Monique Robinson, herself a wounded, fatherless daughter, said,

Honoring our father is tied to long life. Dishonesty toward your father will only hurt *you*. Feeding deep-seated anger, bitterness, and a hardened heart can cause premature death. The *actions* that created the father-daughter wounds don't lead to death. Your father will answer to God for his actions. The father-daughter wounds don't lead to death. The *Father* can heal them. How you *respond* to your father who wounded you will determine what happens to you.[8]

Chapter 11

EASY? NO! REDEEMING? YES!

———

Prodigal—not a pleasant term. It leaves a bad taste in your mouth and a sinking feeling in the pit of your stomach. It's a label given to people who are wasteful and have turned away from their value system. They throw away potential, abilities, health, and relationships. I mention this because of a conversation with Marie. She began by saying, "My father is a prodigal."

"What do you mean by a prodigal? I thought that was a term reserved for children who violate their standards or their parents'?"

"No, not really. Dad turned his back on what he said mattered most to him. He turned his back on Mom and my sister and me. He left, and not only that, he left us destitute financially and relationally. No reason. No explanation. No reaching out, and he doesn't live that far away either. He could have reached out if he wanted to. He didn't. It hurts, and just like the son in the Scripture who took his inheritance, he's a prodigal, but he never came to his senses. He never returned."

"Well, since you mentioned that story in Luke 15, I think there are two other characters in that story. Do you remember who they were?"

"Of course, there was his father and his older brother."

"And how did they respond in the story?"

"Well, the older brother was upset. He was incensed at his

father for letting his brother off so easy and making such a big deal about his return. And the father was quick to forgive. As soon as he saw that his son had wised up, he forgave him."

"So, we have three characters in this story, the prodigal, the father, and the critical elder son. We know who the prodigal is in your story, but which of the remaining two characters do you identify with the most? Which one are you?"

There was silence for a moment, and then Marie spoke, "I'd never thought of that. I just don't think Dad will ever return."

"Does it depend on his returning to determine who we are in the story? We could be responding either way at this time in our heart or mind. Think about it."

"Maybe I'm a mixture. I'm critical of Dad. What he did wasn't fair. I'm angry. He should pay for what he did. But part of me would like to respond like the father in the story. I just wish my father would rush to me and hold me. But the son came back, didn't he, and that's why the father forgave him."

HE SHOULD PAY FOR WHAT HE DID.

"Let's think about this. You're right when you say you're a mixture of the father and the older brother. In fact, I think we all have multiple personalities. Each of us has a prodigal, a loving father, and a critical older brother inside of us. And even though we hope we would respond like a loving father, sometimes the prodigal or the elder brother takes over. Maybe it doesn't always show in our behavior; we could be responding either way in our hearts toward others and in our mind."

Marie thought for a moment and said, "I can see that. I've been all three. But Dad hasn't given me a chance to be the forgiving father, since he's never reached out or come back."

"I don't think it depends on that. In the Bible story the father had a lot to forgive his son for. It wasn't that he just disappointed his father, he had shamed him. He had revolted against his family. To ask for his inheritance was like saying, 'Dad, I wish you were dead.'"

WHY FORGIVE?

Have you ever thought about *when* the father forgave his prodigal son? I think the forgiveness came before his father ever saw him shuffling home. He was forgiven in advance. It wasn't dependent on the response of the son. That would put the father at the mercy of his son's behavior. When he saw his son he welcomed him. If your father were to walk into your life today, would he be welcomed? Would it depend on what he said or did? Would forgiveness have already occurred, or is it held off for some future time?

Why did he forgive his son? Why not? He was his son. He forgave him for his sake and for his own sake as well. We get so wrapped up in looking at what the person did that was so wrong, at the extent of our hurt. I wonder what happens when we stop looking at the wrong and look at the person. The father did. He looked beyond the selfishness, the ungratefulness, and the rebellion and he saw him for who he was—his son. It's the same way God responds to us. He sees our value and provides a way out of our rebellion through the gift of His Son. Just as the prodigal didn't deserve forgiveness, so none of us deserves it. That's what forgiveness is.[1]

Lewis Smedes described this when he said,

> We forgive as we rediscover the person behind the offense, as we surrender our right to revenge, and as we wish good things for the person who did bad things to us, just as the father did. We can forgive before the person who does us wrong comes groveling back, as the father did. We can heal our own spirit, alone, and get the first benefits of forgiving, as he did. We can open ourselves to the possibilities of reunion, as he did.[2]

Your father may never return or return in the way you want him to return. I've talked with some women who were disappointed when their father came back. They were sorry about it.

Remember that your father is human. He is a sinner like we all are. God covers our sin with the blood that Jesus shed on the cross so He won't see our sin, and He washes us with it. He washes us with the blood of the Lamb so that He can see the real us beneath our stains and can focus on the persons He made us (and is remaking us) to be. This is why "Without the shedding of blood there is no forgiveness" (Hebrews 9:22). "In short, He covers up the wrong we *did* so that He can rediscover the persons we *are*."[3]

Many daughters are so locked onto what their father did or didn't do that they never know who their father really is. The best definition of forgiveness is "wishing the other person well." And taking this a step further, "the will of the forgiving father is for all to be well with us and for all of us to be well."[4]

What needs to be done so this occurs between you and your father?

Ask yourself: What do you want? Is it to forgive him? To be reunited? To be reconciled? To be free from bitterness?

Some daughters aren't sure what they want.

Some daughters simply don't want to change, so there's another question to consider. A strange question: "What are you getting out of being estranged from your father? What are the benefits for you?" This is not a judgmental question or one that implies that you shouldn't be where you are in your relationship. But even in a painful situation there may be rewards such as freedom from the pain of Dad's remarks or questions, compassion from others, sympathy, protection, safety, etc. List your reasons:

_____

_____

_____

These reasons could be why you prefer to stay right where you are in the relationship. But let's look at the other side, what we call the price tag. What is this costing you? "What is the price I am paying by not attempting to heal this relationship?"

_____

_____

The next question is not a past issue but a future concern. "How many months or years do I want to continue where I am now?"

_____

_____

It's like asking: "How far into the future do I want my dad's influence to determine what I do with my life? And how will this affect me or cost me?"

Filling Our Suitcases

There's another way to consider what you're presently experiencing. Let's assume you're getting ready for a trip. You're looking forward to it. You bring out the new suitcase. You just purchased this one because it was made of flexible material and you can pack more in it than the others. You begin to select the items you want to accompany you. The piles seem to grow, but you should be able to get everything into it. Your suitcase begins to bulge and expand, but that's what it's supposed to do. Finally you get everything in, sitting on it so you can close the zipper. It doesn't have the same shape it used to, but that's all right. You try to lift it and you can barely budge it. You begin to drag it because that's the only way you can get it to your car and then your destination. Already you're beginning to wonder if you need all this stuff and if it's worth the hassle. The trip is beginning to feel more like a burden than a pleasure.

This is the way it is for many daughters who've been hurt by their fathers. They wake up in the morning and fill a huge suitcase with all the memories of the past, along with the resulting hurts, and then the real stuff is packed: anger, injustices, resentment, and grudges. Some daughters have a mixture of feelings and memories—not only is it what they missed out on but also what they will never have. They itemize how Dad failed them as well as how they've failed themselves. It's just baggage, but by now it's excess baggage. And it's not like you can ship this suitcase on ahead of you. It's handcuffed to you, so you drag it everywhere. It weighs you down, drains your energy, and hinders your progress—and worse yet, you're carrying things you don't even need.[5] All that you're carrying can be summed up in one word—a *grudge*.

Grudge—it's not a nice sounding word, is it? It sits in your throat like a lump. A grudge comes when you've collected injustices that feed anger. It's like an emotional scab that's picked at for so long it gets infected, and the poison begins to move into every area of your life. How do you know if you're carrying a grudge? There's an energy drain. It's used on remembering hurts and keeping score. It's used on rehearsing what you would like to say, and thinking of ways to punish the other person. It's letting anger fester even to the point of rage. You look for ways to initiate a payback. Another way to determine if grudges exist is to look at your physical and emotional health. There is physical fallout to grudges—stress, elevated blood pressure, ulcers, colitis, arthritis, and other ailments.

There is also emotional fallout since we project onto others issues we've had with Dad. Suspicion, hypersensitivity, and negativity are a few of the results. Grudges hurt the person holding them. They're not worth it. They're unbiblical. They will only get you what you don't want in life. There's a much better way.[6]

One of my favorite authors on the subject of forgiveness is Lewis Smedes. Think about his statement on what to do about Dad:

> Forgiving is the only way to heal the wounds of a past we cannot change and cannot forget. Forgiving changes a bitter memory into a grateful memory, a cowardly memory into a courageous memory, an enslaved memory into a free memory, and more than anything else forgiveness gives birth to hope for the future after our past illusions have been shattered.[7]

I've heard many say, "I could forgive if only he would own up to what he did and apologize."

As you think about forgiveness, what are three things you wish your father would apologize for?

1. _____

2. _____

3. _____

What will it do for you if he apologizes?

_____

_____

What will it do for you if he doesn't apologize?

_____

_____

Can you think of three things you need to apologize to your dad for?

1. _____

2. _____

3. _____

If you were to apologize, what would you like to hear in response?

_____

_____

Is there anything else you would like your father to do that would enable you to forgive him?

_____

_____

Over the years I've had the experience of seeing the reconciliation of fathers and their adult daughters. I have seen an emotionally distant adult daughter develop a caring relationship with her aged father. I have seen abused daughters develop a healthy relationship with their fathers through the forgiveness that Jesus Christ allows us to experience. For some of you, when you forgive your father, you will move into a closer relationship with him. For other daughters, you'll forgive your father, but you won't be any closer to him because he will make no effort to change. For some your father has died, but he doesn't have to be alive for you to be free.

There is one way to move ahead in life and to experience God's abundance and grace. It's through forgiveness. Forgiveness is the ultimate step to healing a wound. Yes, it may be difficult. You may not be there yet. You may not feel that your dad deserves forgiveness. But that's what it's all about, isn't it? *None of us deserves it.* It's got to be a gift. It's a gift that will give you freedom. But it's a process. It's slow, and that's all right. Perhaps the first step is working at how you feel about this step. Completing these statements can help you.

Dad, it's difficult for me to forgive you for . . .

_____

_____

_____

I'd like to forgive you for . . .

_____

_____

_____

Writing a Release

One way to formalize your act of forgiveness is to write a statement of release that fits your own personal situation with your father. Here are some statements of release you can use as models for your own statement:

Dad, I release you from determining how I feel and how I respond to others in my life. I release you from the anger and resentment that I have held toward you and others in my life because of you. This includes anger and resentment for . . .

I no longer hold you responsible for my happiness. I release you from my expectations of who you should have been, what you should have done, and . . .

I forgive you for . . .

Dad, I release you for not being there for me emotionally and for your silence over the years. I don't know why you weren't there. I don't need to know.

Dad, I was mad at you for dying when I was a teen and not giving me a chance to get to know you. I missed out on so much. I blamed you. I'm sorry. I hope you're in heaven.

Forgiveness, especially for years of neglect, abandonment, or abuse doesn't come easy. Forgiveness is a process. If you find yourself struggling with expressing positive feelings toward your father, there may be some unresolved resentment still hiding within you. There is a way of uncovering those feelings and clearing the way for your being able to move ahead.

Take a blank sheet of paper and at the top write the salutation "Dear Dad." Under the salutation, write the words "I forgive you for . . ." Then complete the sentence by stating something your father did that has bothered you all these years. For example, "I forgive you for not affirming me."

The next step is to identify the first thought you experience after writing your sentence. It may be a rebuttal to the forgiveness you're trying to express. It may be an emotional protest against what you've written. For example, the woman who is forgiving her father for not affirming her may remember how he made fun of her when she dressed up on Sundays, or made light of it whenever she accomplished something. This thought brings her resentment to the surface.

Whatever your thought might be, write another "I forgive you for . . ." statement for it. Keep writing "I forgive you for . . ." statements for every thought that comes to the surface. Don't be discouraged if your angry protests contradict the desire to learn to forgive, or if they're so strong that it seems like you have not expressed any forgiveness at all. Remember, you're in the *process* of forgiving your father. Continue to write until all the pockets of resentment and resistance have been drained.

Some complete this process with only a few statements. Others have more resentment to clear away, and they continue writing for several pages. You will know you have completed your work when you write "I forgive you for . . ." and can't think of any more responses to complete the statement.

After you have finished writing, sit facing an empty chair and read your statements of forgiveness aloud. Imagine your father sitting there, accepting your forgiveness with both verbal and nonverbal affirmation. Take as long as you need for this step, explaining and amplifying your statements as you go if necessary. I sat and listened to such a reading in my office for fifteen minutes one day.

Don't show this list to anyone. It's not necessary. When you're finished verbalizing your statements, destroy the entire list. Burn it or tear it into little pieces, symbolizing that "the old has gone, the new has come!" (2 Corinthians 5:17).

LETTING GO

Forgiveness involves letting go. It's like holding a pen tightly in your hand, opening your hand, and watching it drop to the floor. Remember playing tug-of-war as a child? As long as the parties on each end of the rope are tugging, you have a "war." But when someone lets go, the war is over. When you forgive your father, you are letting go of your end of the rope. No matter how hard he may tug on the other end, if you have released your end, the war is over for you.

At some point you need to accept the reality of who your father was and is. When you were young you may have thought that your father knew what he was doing. You could have believed that he new what was right and wrong. Perhaps most of the time he did what was right, but perhaps he didn't. Your father had his own difficult background and personal deficits, and these have probably impacted you. Without excusing his behavior, you need to let go of those negative experiences by forgiving him. It's the only method of ending the war between the two of you that you have control over. If you continue to hang on, you're letting what happened control you.

Don't Forget to Forgive Yourself

There is one other step you may not be expecting. You may need to forgive yourself. But why forgive yourself? There are several reasons. You may be blaming yourself and feeling guilty for:

1. not being able to change—or cure—your father for whatever problem he had;
2. not living up to his expectations for you, no matter how unreasonable they may have been;
3. not being loved and accepted by him (you may have felt it was because of a defect in your appearance or personality);
4. not being perfect in some way, or in every way;
5. treating yourself the way your father treated you (identify how you may have done this);
6. mistreating yourself when you have difficult times as a result of your past;
7. choosing men like your father in hopes that you can reform them;
8. developing some of the same tendencies or problems you despised in your father.

Isn't it ironic that we often take out our frustrations on ourselves rather than on the person who hurt us? Perhaps we consider ourselves a safer target than the person we are struggling with. If your father has hurt you in the past, you may feel that you can't vent your frustration on him because he'll only hurt you again. So you take the path of least resistance by shouldering the blame. This isn't necessary. It wasn't before and it's not now.[8]

Forgiveness is a medicine for pain. It heals the pain of a wounded memory and the hole in the heart as well as seething rage, resentment, and the chokehold of hate.

Forgiveness happens within you. It's completed in your head and mind. It means you see your father as worthy of your love. Do you?

Jan asked, "If I forgive my father does that mean I have to spend time with him? I don't want to be bitter, but he hasn't changed. He hasn't acknowledged what he's done. I don't even want to see him. I don't want a reunion." There is a big difference between forgiveness and a reunion. Lewis Smedes describes the difference:

It takes one person to forgive.
It takes two to be reunited.

REUNION HAS

Forgiving happens inside the wounded person.

SEVERAL

STRINGS

Reunion happens in a relationship between people.

ATTACHED.

We can forgive a person who never says he's sorry.

We cannot be truly reunited unless he is honestly sorry.

We can forgive even if we do not trust the person who wronged us once not to wrong us again.

Reunion can happen only if we can trust the person who wronged us once not to wrong us again.

Forgiving has no strings attached.

Reunion has several strings attached.[9]

One daughter described how she and her siblings went to their father's funeral and celebrated her father's life. He had been an angry, frustrated man and sexually molested his children.

This is what she said:

We walked away from his coffin knowing that he would rest in peace, and even more important, that we would go on living at peace with ourselves.

What made the difference for us? Forgiveness.

Perhaps you are shaking your head in disbelief right now and wondering how anyone could truly forgive something as unspeakable as incest. You may be asking yourself why any-one would want to. The truth is we did not want to. We did not set out to forgive. All we ever wanted was for the pain from the past to stop interfering with our lives and our happiness in the present. To accomplish that, my sister, my brother, and I, each in our own way, worked through our pain and let go of it.

We did not and never will forget what happened to us. We did not and never will condone our father's actions. Nothing could alter the fact that how he treated us was no way to treat little kids. Yet before our dad died, according to our own time frames, each of us reached a point where we no longer needed to make him pay for what he had done. We stopped expecting him to make up for it. We stopped using incest as an excuse for everything that was wrong with our lives. And we stopped waiting for our parents to give us as adults what we did not receive from them as children. We let go. We healed. And yes, we forgave.[10]

Listen to the response of a daughter to the survey question "At this point in your life what would you like to be able to say to your father?" Her words are what many have been able to do:

I love you and forgive you! Dad, we have been through a lot together, and I know that you tried your best. I know now that I required different things and had different needs than my brother and sisters. Thank you for recognizing that and asking for my forgiveness this past year. Yes, you were not always there for me emotionally and spiritually, but you only acted in that way because you knew no better. Your parents were exactly the same way. I was hurt and angry with you for a long time, and through therapy and the love of Christ

I can forgive you and move forward. I harbor no ill feelings and truly have peace about our relationship as it stands now. I feel comfortable with you and no longer fear your disapproval or anger. Only as an adult—I can now see that you did love me in your own way. It may not have been the way I would have loved a child, but it was your way and I accept that. We have proven to many that it is not too late to mend the hurt and pain and start anew.

Thank you for your honesty when I was at Remunda (E.D. Christian Facility) this past year. You showed more emotions in three days than I saw in my lifetime. You were amazing. Thank you for recognizing the pain I felt. Thank you for your forgiveness of the abortions I had and my bad judgments. I want you to know that I love our relationship now and the fact that I can talk to you about anything. I really feel comfortable, and value your opinions. You are intelligent, honest, and have a lifetime of experience. I can respect your feedback and advice. I love you and thank you for not giving up on me. You are an amazing father, and I only hope that I make you as proud as you have made me. You finally came around, and I thank God for all the blessings He has bestowed on our relationship. Please forgive me for the pain that I caused you. I was not always the perfect child and did not appreciate the things you did for me as much as I could have. I am sorry for the suicide attempt and the hurt that you felt because of my selfishness. I am sorry for not being honest with you about my eating disorder and lying to you. I am sorry if you felt that I have failed you in any way.

It's never too late to pray for your father, if he's still living. Begin to pray now, perhaps in a new way. Pray about his weaknesses, pray for his growth, and ask God's blessing upon his life. The best step you can take is to release your past and your father to the Lord. Pray about the possibility of a new relationship that could occur. Pray for the Lord's renewing strength. Ask Him to incorporate into your life how He sees you. God sees your father in the same way—worthy, valued, and a "new creation."[11]

A Step Further

I would like you to consider something very different. It's a prayer of praise for you and your father—it may take you some time before you can pray this, and that's all right. The day will come.

Dear Lord,

I praise You for your act of choosing my father and me, adopting us, and making us your heirs. Thank you for forgiving our sins and sealing us with your Holy Spirit.

Thank You that Dad and I are never out of your mind.

Thank You for not being disillusioned about us.

Thank You for your continuing determination about us.

Thank You for the never-ending joy you have over Dad and me.

Saturate me with the truth of who You are and what I am becoming because of my identity in You.

I pray that the way I live my life will reflect the value You place on me. I pray that I will draw others to open their lives to You. May they be able to discover what You have done for them.

In Jesus' name,
Amen.

Chapter 12

WHO IS YOUR REAL FATHER?

Jesus said to pray in this manner: "Our father . . ." When you pray those first two words is it comfortable, awkward, fulfilling, or difficult even to say them? Someone has said, "My relationship with my father was so damaging that to this day I can't hear anyone pray to God without an involuntary cringe." How sad for that to be the case. Your father can have a tremendous impact upon you concerning your belief in God the Father and your personal relationship with Jesus Christ. In our survey we asked the question "How has your relationship with your father affected your relationship with God and with Jesus?" Here are some of the responses from adult daughters who had positive relationships with their fathers and from those who had difficult ones. See which ones you can identify with as they share from their hearts.

"I have always longed to be loved by a male figure. I often see myself dancing before the Lord as a child, and He is smiling and delighting in me. As much as I know the Lord loves me—I also am not sure He will protect me."

"I became very suspicious of God because I feared He was cruel like my father. I felt worthless and unlovable."

"The hardest thing for me to 'get' was that I didn't have to do works to get God's love. I had to learn unconditional love for the first time. When things go wrong in my life, I still have to realize it's not always punishment but just life in an imperfect world. I have had to learn grace to break free from shame."

"My father controlled me spiritually throughout my life. I had to think and believe the way my dad told me to, and I could not explore my own relationship with God. I grew to hate God and became very suspicious of Him. I viewed God as abusive, just as my dad was. I knew a lot of Bible verses and understood the 'steps' to becoming a Christian. However, I was deeply rebellious toward God and felt tremendous rage at Him for abandoning me. I used to lie in bed at night and silently blame God for my troubles. I saw Jesus as a victim of child abuse at the hands of His father in the same way I was."

"My father was never one to initiate prayer or Bible study together. We went to church and that was it. As an adult I have learned a relationship with God and Jesus [requires] *much more!*"

I TURNED MY BACK ON GOD.

"I turned my back on God for over thirty years. [I felt that] all men and God wanted [from me was] submission, control, and superficial love. Such anger I had. I didn't even like to think about Jesus. His sacrifice was so great, but I was bad, angry, hateful, disrespectful. Why would He love me? My stepdad had many talents and good qualities, but not for raising little girls. And for what he did to my sister, I hope he is burning in hell."

"My Dad loved the Lord, and when I watched my Dad draw his last breaths I knew, without a doubt, he was in the arms of Jesus. Dad had a sense of pure peace."

"Because I had such a loving relationship [with my dad] I found it easy to believe I had a loving heavenly Father."

"It helped bring me to Jesus. But I have also struggled with seeing God, the Father, as distant and unpredictable. It has been a hard road for me to trust in God's goodness and faithfulness. I have found myself many times trying to earn God's love, and always falling short. I am beginning to understand what unconditional [love] really means."

"Since my dad was so unconditionally accepting of me, and was easy on me growing up, I'm afraid I took God's love for granted for a long time and didn't have a proper awe and realization of the balance between God's love and His righteous judgment. My dad read to my mother and me every day from the Bible and led a short devotional. He made me sit through it all during my teenage rebelliousness, which I hated at the time, but now I realize he modeled for me the faithful discipline of a true believer."

Let's say *you* were given the ability to create the perfect father. There are no limits. What would he be like? I've asked this question and received various answers:

"I don't think I would change anything about the way my father was. I couldn't have asked for a better dad."

"I would have a father who was there—just there in every which way."

"I have no idea of what I would create. I didn't know my dad, and my girlfriends didn't have one either."

One daughter who didn't have a dad in her home said this is what an ideal father would be:

A father is a protector, provider, teacher, and someone who loves me. He is someone to whom I am special and whose focus is on nurturing and caring for me. He protects me from harm. He provides me with his best, delighting and taking pleasure in surprises that show his sensitivity and attention to my needs. He shares himself, teaching me how to live, how to work, how to talk, how to laugh, how to be all I can be. He sees potential and takes time with me to develop character within. He expects good things from me. He directs, counsels, and communicates my uniqueness to me, building inner security.[1]

There is a father in Scripture whom every daughter would love to have. His name is Jairus, a well-known man, an official in the synagogue. "He threw himself down at Jesus' feet and begged him to go to his home, because his only daughter, who was twelve years old, was dying" (Luke 8:41–42 TEV).

At that time in history this is not what a leader or any man would ordinarily do concerning a daughter. A public display over a daughter was shocking in a culture where fathers were publicly proud only of sons. The psalmist said, "The sons a man has when he is young are like arrows in a soldier's hand. Happy is the man who has many such arrows" (Psalm 127:4–5 TEV). A man would go out of his way to help a son, but usually not a daughter. Jairus's act was very humbling, his devotion deeper than his pride. He accepted his own limitations and gave up his independence and self-reliance and said, "Help." In a way he was letting go of his daughter and saying, "I can't do it. I need God's help." He would do anything to save his daughter.[2]

A TRULY PERFECT FATHER

There is only one perfect father and he's not an earthly father. But for some he, too, is hard to trust. Often a woman's image of God is a replica of the image she had of her earthly father. If her father was less than ideal, she could develop a distorted image of God the Father. We allow others to twist our image of God. Experiences with your earthly father interfere with just about everything.

The hunger a daughter has for her father can be filled by our heavenly Father. God can be depended on. He is who He says He is. If a daughter's view of God has been polluted by her earthly father, she needs to begin telling herself that there's no comparison between the two. Too often a snap judgment is made about God without bothering to investigate who He really is. If God is like your earthly father, then He isn't God, is He? Remember, you won't fully understand Him *because* He is God. He's too big, too wise, too kind, too just, too loving, and too perfect for us to get our minds around Him completely.

When you look at how the Scriptures describe God, you see that He has many names that reflect His role as our parent. If any human father could provide all of the following, he really would be a wonderful father. All the names are connected to the name *Jehovah,* which means "God is the only ever-living One, the only living One," and "the self-existent One."

Ponder some examples of God's name and see how aptly they describe His role as a perfect parent for us.

- Jehovah-Jireh, "the Lord provides"
- Jehovah Raphe, "the Lord who heals you"
- Jehovah-M'Kaddesh, "the God who makes you holy"
- Jehova-Raki, "God who is our Shepherd"

His parenting skills cover it all!

Sometimes we have humanized God too much. We have created Him into the image *we* want to have of God. Isn't it interesting that we let our earthly father define what our heavenly Father is like? Shouldn't it be the other way around? Shouldn't we start with God our heavenly Father and model after Him what a godly father should be? Then perhaps we wouldn't assume God is like our earthly father. A small daughter who has a long-distance father needs to know that isn't the way it's supposed to be. She needs to know that God is close, always there at all times. And it's not based on her feelings, either. One woman whose father died when she was an infant said, "God could not be like my real father, because my real father was not there. I had no frame of references when I thought about God. I thought of him as a 'Holy Other.' There was not enough skin on God."[3]

God Makes the Difference

I'd like you to hear the insights of a mother whose husband was killed in a tragic accident. She was single for nine years, raising two young daughters.

A daughter without a dad will have to spend time with the Lord praying, meditating, and seeking His will. She will need to maintain spiritual disciplines with a new attitude of hunger in her heart. Her heart needs to ask God to reveal himself as her Father.

I am over forty and have to fight to make this thought a reality. I was a single parent for nine years. I am an only child, and my father doesn't yet know the Lord. I have to mentally put my father aside and listen to my heavenly Father. Often what I hear from my earthly father conflicts with what God tells me. Yet what I hear from God— through His Word, through thoughts that come to me in prayer, through the counsel of His people, and through the evidences of His leading in my life and the spiritual discernment He gives me—is sufficient to guide and comfort me.

Even with many years of pulling from all these resources, I have to make a conscious effort to keep a secure reality of God as my Father. My commitment to knowing more about God, and my requests to Him to show me how He is my Father, [are manifested] in the reality of His presence in my life.

My daughters have been without their father since they were seven and ten years old, and they have had to face the same challenge. My older daughter is a very practical young woman. It seems harder for her to rely on God than it does for my younger daughter. She is capable and independent, and has learned how to survive without a father in a responsible way. She continually struggles to discipline her mind, open her heart, and allow God to participate in her life as her Father.

God is our Father. He is with her at her basketball game.

He is with me as I make decisions that need fatherly counsel. Practically speaking, we don't always feel that He is here. But that doesn't change the fact that He is.

God goes to school plays and sporting events and proms. He is there in the middle of the night when loneliness seems to suffocate, and in the middle of the day when pressures of life make frantic demands.

He makes a difference in a life. He sees, hears, touches, and feels the pain and He stays.[4]

Dads Bring Both Joy and Sorrow

In your journey of moving on in your relationship with your earthly father, remember this: Even in the midst of difficult and painful times with a father, there can be positives. Too often we lock our focus onto one facet and miss another. It's not always either/or. Just like joy and sorrow are not on a continuum but a mixture existing at the same time, so will your experiences with your father be a mixture. You just have to look for them as this daughter did:

Now that my dad is older, he's mellowed. He's becoming the father that I always wanted him to be. During his years of alcoholism, it was awful. He was a big-time perfectionist and overachiever. This is the odd thing about my dad. Even though he was abusive in some ways, my father taught me that I was smart enough to do anything I set my mind to do. So I grew up believing I had no limitations. That's probably the greatest gift he gave me.

Now that he's sober, he's a very different person. He says "I love you" first now. He talks about his feelings. He's really mellowed. He's working to undo some of the damage he caused, especially with my brother, who has had the hardest time with him. I am grateful for the legacy that my dad has given me. I am very strong-willed and opinionated. My intelligence, my confidence, and my drive are all things that I have gotten from him.[5]

Another daughter talked about her father, who left his wife with five children to raise with no support for four years. He came back, and then left again for four years. She stated she hated him, and then he returned when she was in junior high and began to build the family, enrolling in college himself. She said,

I've come to see that he thought he was doing his best. He's always loved us and knows he missed out on the biggest part of our lives. Today I can honestly say that I loved him, and respect the fact that he never gave up on us, even when we did on him.

Now he and I talk on a different level—about life, marriage, careers, and aspirations. Without those good and bad experiences in my life, I would be a different person than I am today. My dad showed me that whatever comes my way, deal with it the best you can and it will work out in the end. Try not to look at the world so pessimistically, but from different angles, because things aren't always what they seem at first glance. Go beyond what's given to you, because nothing is really given to you, it's blessed upon you.[6]

DON'T GIVE UP THE DREAM

As we come to the end of this book, I wanted to leave you with some examples of positive relationships between daughters and their dads and some incidences of genuine reconciliation that came out of very difficult situations. I do this to give you hope that even difficult fathers can change and to let you know there are many dads who *are* coming through with love and acceptance for their daughters. If you're married and have daughters, perhaps you can encourage your husband to give himself to them. His role is so significant. Don't let him forget that!

More words from daughters about their fathers:

"Though I grew up in a time when most families didn't say 'I love you' very often, I instinctively knew that it was true [in my dad's case], even though in hindsight he never came to any of my school functions (never an issue to me then, in contrast to today's soccer moms and 'sports-parents syndrome'). But if I ever had gotten into 'kid trouble,' I was fully aware I would get the lecture of my life, an appropriate consequence, and full acceptance back into the bosom of the family. My father's consistent love, consistent discipline, and consistent example are probably the most significant factors in keeping me out of any major kid trouble and in shaping me into the person I am today."

"He was always there to listen and to care. To him I was funny, delightful. I always knew I was loved. Still do."

"My father was my anchor growing up. My mother had mental problems so my father and I became a united front to keep our sanity, but also to help her. There was nothing my father and I didn't discuss. He valued my opinion and

MY FATHER WAS MY ANCHOR

I valued his. My father and I were so close that my mother would ask me to talk to my father when she was having trouble understanding his viewpoint. As I became an adult my father pulled back and expected me to make my own decisions. I hated that. My father had a wonderful sense of humor. If there is one thing I would like to thank my father for, that would be uppermost. It has helped me see life in a better perspective. Not to take situations and myself so seriously."

"He has always given me the benefit of the doubt, even when there were times I had broken his trust (when I was a teenager). He allowed me to rebuild that trust and form the relationship we have now that I am an adult. He has always worked hard to give me a good life, and would bend over backward to help me if ever I needed him. He is a great encourager, gives great advice, and gentle criticism."

"My father has been there to support me and advise me and help me out in so many ways that it's difficult to know where to begin. When I was little he made every effort to get to my piano recitals and school performances, even though his evening schedule was pretty busy. He's helped me financially in ways that I can never repay. He has helped me move from one location to another enough times that he should by all rights have a very bad back by now. He has answered about a million faith/religion/theology questions for me over the years. And most important, he has been a prayer warrior for me and someone I know I can always turn to for any kind of support as long as he is alive and well."

"My father has been the greatest spiritual and emotional mentor in my life. He always challenges me to think deeper about my faith and reflect on the greatness of God and the complexities and wonder of the Christian journey. He taught me how to take responsibility for my emotions and reactions to life's circumstances, and how to reason objectively when I'd rather let my feelings control my responses. He spent a great deal of time with my sister and me on daddy-daughter dates. I got a lot of hugs and kisses and felt special when he took time to hang out and be silly with me. He taught me not to take myself too seriously, but to enjoy every day. We laugh and have a great time together!"

"Though he traveled a lot during my childhood years, when he was home, I felt that our family was the most important thing in his life—we played, and camped, and just enjoyed one another's company. When I was in eighth grade, and he saw how repeated moves that enabled him to climb up the corporate (in his case, government) ladder were crushing my spirit (having to make new friends every eighteen months can do that to an introverted adolescent), he committed not to move again until all his kids were out of high school— and he stuck to that promise. That is the biggest thing I remember about growing up with my dad—he had integrity. His yes meant yes. I never had to wonder if he would keep his word. Others knew that about him too, and it made me proud, and it made me want to be just like him. Another thing that gave me an incredible sense of security in my life was that we all knew that our parents prayed for us in bed every night. It was so comforting to hear the rumble of their prayers (it was easy to distinguish between parental conversation and prayers) through the bedroom walls. I knew that my parents had their priorities in the right place and that they were petitioning God on our behalf."

Unexpected Gifts and Graces

For years my wife Joyce and I considered our retarded son, Matthew, a tremendous source of blessing in our lives. Our values, perspective on life, character qualities, insight, skills, and relationship with God were all refined and increased because of the presence of this handicapped child.

On March 15, 1990, Matthew was called home to be with the Lord. We felt an extremely empty place in our family. Parents rarely expect to outlive their children. All we have left of Matthew are precious memories. So anything that adds to that storehouse is highly valued. Because of the severity of his retardation, Matthew was only able to speak a few words and had very few responses. We had only one brief film of him and no audio recordings. At his death, he was still only about eighteen months old mentally.

August 15, 1991 arrived—the day Matthew would have observed his twenty-fourth birthday. Any anniversary is painful when the loss is fresh. But that evening we contacted an attendant who had cared for Matthew at Salem Christian Home, his residence for the last eleven years of his life. A friend had told us that this woman wanted to tell us some of her experiences with Matthew.

As we talked with this attendant over the phone, she shared with us several aspects of Matthew's life we had never seen. She described how he had learned to put together a very simple puzzle. When she took him for a walk outside, Matthew would walk way ahead and then try to hide from her. She shared how he had learned to dry his own hair with a hair dryer, and how he would turn it around and blow it on her hair. One day she brought her own six-month-old baby into the dorm for all the residents to see. She sang "Rock-a-Bye Baby", as Matthew held this little baby in his arms, and she noticed tears running down our son's face.

To someone who has never gone through the experience of

raising a handicapped child, this might not seem like much. But when the limitations are so massive and the ordinary experiences of life so few, knowing these additional experiences of our son were immeasurable blessings for us.

I never cease to marvel at God's timing. The very next day, I received a letter from a woman who had written me a year earlier. Her first letter described how a healing had taken place between her and her eighty-three-year-old father. A rift between them for a quarter of a century had been mended, and a new bonding had occurred. She wanted to share this with me because my book *Always Daddy's Girl* had helped her with this relationship. She also asked if I would pray for her father who hadn't yet invited Jesus Christ into his life, to be his personal Savior.

In this new letter which I received, this woman shared how her father had indeed become a Christian the year before. What an encouragement for us who had prayed for him! She then went on to say that he had died just three months later. In her letter she enclosed a written portrayal of one of her last visits with him. I share it here with her permission because it provides a beautiful picture of the passages of life through which we all move in our parent/child relationships.

Examples of father-daughter reconciliation come from unexpected places. This one touched our hearts:

Mid-life. A reversal of roles. Dad is the child now and I am the parent.

We got word that his heart was failing. He made a valiant effort to come to his granddaughter's wedding, but the trip proved to be too much for him. Upon arrival at the wedding, he looked ashen gray. Everyone was concerned about him. I reassured myself that with a little rest next week he would be fine. But next week came, and along with it the alarming news. He was listless, unable to be aroused at times, pale and trembling, and his legs and ankles were very swollen. All symptoms of congestive heart failure.

As a daughter, my heart was heavy with the thought of

losing Dad. Tears flowed freely as I prayed for another opportunity to be with him before he died. How I longed to tell him one more time how much he meant to me. You see, our relationship now as father and daughter was a very simple yet tender one. Each time I visited him, I would remind him that he gave out hugs like no one else could, and that I still needed him to be my dad. His face always beamed when he was reminded.

When packing my bags to make the four-hour journey to his home, thoughts turned to a book that I had recently given to my daughters. It was a children's book that told how love is passed from one generation to another. I tucked it into my suitcase, hoping to be able to share it with Dad.

Upon arriving, the doctor confirmed our suspicion—it was congestive heart failure. Dad could have another heart attack at any moment. The doctor requested that I stay with him for the next week to monitor his condition.

The second evening, after dinner, I told Dad that I wanted to share something with him—a story about him and me. He responded appreciatively to my request to read the story to him. As I began to read, emotion engulfed my voice. The story began with the child as a baby being rocked in the arms of the parent and having this song sung to him:

I'll love you forever
I'll like you for always
As long as I'm living
My baby you'll be.

As the story unfolded of the child passing through the various stages of childhood into maturity, Dad listened with enjoyment. At every stage of development, the parent would sing the same verse to the child. He looked at the pictures with childlike eagerness, commenting on them every now and then. At that moment came the realization that our roles had been reversed. I was now the parent, reading a story to the child. It felt strange. But it was all right, for that's the way life is sometimes. Roles do change as we pass from one stage of life into another.

In the story, years after the child reached maturity, the parent became elderly and frail. The picture showed a frowning man holding his dying mother in his arms, rocking her and singing this song:

I'll love you forever
I'll like you for always
As long as I'm living
My mother you'll be.

"That's how I feel about you, Dad. I will love you forever!" Tears filled both our eyes, and he hugged me once again.

The days of our visit quickly passed, and it was time to make the four-hour return trip home. My family was expecting me for dinner that evening. It would be difficult to leave Dad, knowing that I might never see him again this side of heaven. But the Lord had already assured me that someday in heaven, we will be reunited. Now my calling as a parent will be to go back home to the next generation and pass on the song that Dad has sung to me in every stage of life:

I'll love you forever
I'll like you for always
As long as I'm living
My baby you'll be.[7]

POSTSCRIPT

We've traveled over a lot of road together. We've looked at the impact that your earthly father had—and continues to have—in your life. We've seen how that important relationship can shape how you approach the world and interact with other people.

We've also explored ways that we can come to terms with our loss and allow ourselves the freedom to grieve. Some of you have bravely faced the disappointments of your past and have decided to no longer let them determine your future happiness.

The most important message of this book—the one that I hope you will take with you—is the fact that you do have a perfect Father who will never leave you, never forsake you, and never disappoint you. No matter how disappointing your first father relationship was, its sting can pale in comparison to the awesome love that your heavenly Father wants to lavish on you. Allow Him to fill the emptiness you may feel.

If you feel that there is still much that you need to process and work through, don't hesitate to seek out a godly counselor who can help you take the important steps necessary to make healing a reality in your life. There is no shame in taking advantage of all the resources that God has provided for us. He wants to see you healed, restored, and getting on with the joy of living.

Here is my parting prayer for you, taken from Ephesians 3:16–19 (TLB):

That out of his glorious, unlimited resources he [God] will give you the mighty inner strengthening of his Holy Spirit. And I pray that Christ will be more and more at home in your hearts, living within you as you trust in him. May your roots go down deep into the soil of God's marvelous love; and may you be able to feel and understand . . . how long, how wide, how deep, and how high his love really is; and to experience this love for yourselves, though it is so great that you will never see the end of it. . . . And so at last you will be filled up with God himself.

ENDNOTES

Chapter One
1. Michael Gurian, *The Wonder of Girls* (New York: Atria Books, 2002), 156–58.
2. Patrick Morley and David Delk, *The Dad in the Mirror* (Grand Rapids, Mich.: Zondervan, 2003), adapted, 44–49.
3. Rick Warren, *The Purpose-Driven Life* (Grand Rapids, Mich.: Zondervan, 2002), 22–24.

Chapter Two
1. Joe Kelly, *Dads and Daughters* (New York: Broadway Books, 2003), 6.
2. Ibid., adapted, 12–18.
3. Ibid., adapted, 11.
4. Dewitt Henry and James McPhearson, eds., *Fathering Daughters* (Boston: Beacon Press Books, 1998), adapted, 188–98.
5. Ibid., 193, 204.
6. Dr. Linda Nielsen, *Embracing Your Father* (New York: McGraw Hill, 1986), 72.
7. Ibid., adapted, 73.

Chapter Three
1. Laura Davis, *I Thought We'd Never Speak Again* (New York: Quill, 2002), adapted, 7.

2. Ibid., 7.
3. Dr. Dan B. Allender, *The Wounded Heart* (Colorado Springs: NavPress, 1995), 30.
4. Ibid., 36.
5. Randy L. Carlson, *Father Memories* (Chicago: Moody, 1992), 13.
6. Jane Myers Drew, Ph.D., *Where Were You When I Needed You, Dad?* (Newport Beach, Calif.: Tiger Lily Publishing, 2003), adapted, 16.
7. Lee Ezell in Gloria Gaither, *What My Parents Did Right* (Nashville: Starsong, 1991), 218.
8. Patricia Love, *The Emotional Incest Syndrome* (New York: Bantam Books, 1990), adapted, 38–50.
9. Shanna Smith, MSW, *Making Peace With Your Adult Children* (New York: Harper Perennial, 1991), adapted, 96–110.

Chapter Four
1. Jonetta Rose Barras, *Whatever Happened to Daddy's Little Girl?* (New York: Ballantine Publishing, 2000), 56.
2. Ibid., 60.
3. Beth M. Erickson, Ph.D., *Longing for Dad: Father Loss and Its Impact* (Deerfield Beach, Fla.: Health Communications, Inc.), 1998.
4. Diane Weathers, *Essence,* as quoted in Barras, *Whatever Happened to Daddy's Little Girl,* 115.
5. Ibid., adapted, 67–72.
6. Ibid., adapted, 73.
7. Elizabeth Fischel, *The Men in Our Lives* (New York: William Morrow, 1985), 50–51.
8. Lois Mowday, *Daughters Without God* (Nashville: Oliver/Nelson, 1990), adapted, 63–64.
9. Erickson, *Longing for Dad,* adapted, 78.
10. Barbara Goulier and Joan Minnenger, Ph.D., *The Father Daughter Dance* (New York: G. P. Putnam and Sons, 1993), adapted, 37–40.

Chapter Five
1. Kyle D. Pruett, M.D., *Fatherhood* (New York: Free Press, 2000), 111.

2. Diane Fassel, Ph.D., *Growing Up Divorced* (New York: Pocket Books, 1991), adapted, 72–116; 126–42.

Chapter Six

1. Adapted from Carolyn Koons, *Beyond Betrayal* (San Francisco: Harper & Row, 1982), 272–73.
2. Maxine Harris, *The Loss That Is Forever* (New York: A Plume Book, 1995), adapted, 4.
3. Ibid., adapted, 15.
4. Ibid., adapted, 38.
5. Arthur Ashe, *Days of Grace* (New York: Alfred Knopf, 1998), 304, as quoted in Maxine Harris, *The Loss That Is Forever* (New York: A Plume Book, 1995), 28–29.
6. Elyse Wakerman, *Father Loss* (New York: Henry Holt & Co., 1984), 13.
7. Gloria Vanderbilt, *Once Upon a Time* (New York: Ballantine, 1985), 31.
8. Harris, *The Loss That Is Forever*, 97.
9. Lois Akner, *How to Survive the Loss of a Parent* (New York: William Morrow, 1993), 8.
10. Judith Wallerstein and Sandra Blakeslee, *Second Chances* (New York: Tichner & Fields, 1989), 13.
11. Love, *The Emotional Incest Syndrome*, adapted, 180–82.

Chapter Seven

1. Pauline Boss, *Ambiguous Loss* (Cambridge, Mass.: Harvard University Press, 1999), adapted, 7–12, 45.
2. David Hart, "The Path to Wholeness," *Psychological Perspective* (Fall 1972), 152.
3. Dr. David Stoop, Ph.D., *Making Peace With Your Father* (Ventura, Calif.: Regal Books, 2004), 199–200.
4. Ibid., adapted, 187–211.
5. Joyce Rupp, *Praying Our Good-byes* (New York: Ivey Books, 1988), 20–21.

Chapter Eight

1. Dr. Sidney B. Simon and Suzanne Simon, *Forgiveness* (New York: Warner Books, 1991), adapted, 102–10.

2. Susan Farward, *Toxic Parents* (New York: Bantam, 1989), adapted, 217–18.
3. Simon and Simon, *Forgiveness*, adapted, 86–95.
4. Ibid., 96.
5. Ibid., adapted, 97–98.

Chapter Nine

1. Dr. Phillip C. McGraw, *Relationship Rescue* (New York: Hyperion, 2000), 41–42.
2. Simon and Simon, *Forgiveness*, adapted, 202–203.
3. Love, *The Emotional Incest Syndrome*, adapted, 172.
4. Ibid., adapted, 178–80.

Chapter Ten

1. Dr. David Stoop, *Forgiving Our Parents, Forgiving Ourselves* (Ann Arbor, Mich.: Servant Publications, 1991), 183–85.
2. Mowday, *Daughters Without God* (Nashville: Oliver/Nelson, 1990), 103.
3. *Oswald Chambers: The Best From All His Books*, Harry Verplaugh, ed. (Nashville: Oliver/Nelson, 1985), 75.
4. Henri Nouwen, *The Living Reminder: Service and Prayer in Memory of Jesus Christ* (New York: Seabury Press, 1977), 19.
5. Ibid., 22.
6. Monique Robinson, *Longing for Daddy* (Colorado Springs: Waterbrook Press, 2004), adapted, 163.
7. Ibid., 2–3.
8. Ibid., adapted, 16.

Chapter Eleven

1. Lewis Smedes, *The Art of Forgiving* (Nashville: Moorings, 1996), adapted, 117–23.
2. Ibid., 125.
3. Ibid., 126.
4. Ibid., 127.
5. Simon and Simon, *Forgiveness*, adapted, 43.
6. Ibid., adapted, 46.
7. Smedes, *The Art of Forgiving*, 176.

8. H. Norman Wright, *Always Daddy's Girl* (Ventura, Calif.: Regal Books, 1989), adapted, 234–37.

9. Smedes, *The Art of Forgiving*, 27.

10. Simon and Simon, *Forgiveness*, adapted, 2–3.

11. Wright, *Always Daddy's Girl*, adapted, 240–41.

Chapter Twelve

1. Lynda Elliott and Vicki Tanner, Ph.D., *My Father's Child* (Brentwood, Tenn.: Wolgemuth & Hyatt, 1988), 98.

2. Gordon Dalbey, *Healing the Masculine Soul* (Dallas: Word Publishing, 1988), adapted, 57.

3. Mowday, *Daughters Without God*, 85.

4. Ibid., 52–53.

5. Carmen Renee Berry and Lynn Barrington, *Daddies and Daughters* (New York: Fireside-Simon & Schuster, 1998), 250–51.

6. Ibid., 253.

7. Letter reprinted by permission of Sherrie Eldridge, Indianapolis, Indiana. Quotation from Robert Munsch, *Love You Forever* (Willowdale, Ontario, Canada: Firefly Books, 1986), 1, 23.

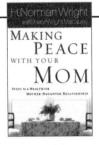